TO.

CHARiE

FiRE BCRMiNg

J. K.O. (signature)

ENgO

THE DEBT COLLECTOR

SHAUN SMITH

CHAPTER 1
THE FIRE

I loved my nan, Annie. We shared a room in a small terrace house in Kirkdale, Liverpool, on Vesuvius Place. It was a bit cramped in there with me, my four brothers and Mum and Dad, too. Nan was partly disabled and I'd do anything for her as we all would. She was the calm one in the family. When something kicked off between us lads, she was the one to settle things down – she always had the right words to say.

Like everyone else when we were kids, Saturday was a big day. It was a chance to go into town and spend what bit of money we had. I used to take Nan with me because she loved browsing and picking up a few pieces. 'Cos she was a bit iffy on her feet, she found it hard to get around, though. She could have used a wheelchair, but she hated the thing. She was too proud for her own good sometimes.

I remember this one afternoon like it was yesterday. We were in town for a few hours and Nan was getting tired so we decided to call it a day and get the bus home. We came out of Littlewoods and I left her for a few seconds to grab the local paper, the Liverpool Echo. Anyway, I just bought me paper when I heard this loud "thud". I turned round and there was Nan, sprawled on the floor with some people bending over her. The poor old girl had slipped and smashed straight into a window, and was on the ground covered in blood. She was in a hell of a state. All I thought was why I'd left her alone – she'd been tired and I really should have stayed with her.

Some of the people beside her were wiping away the blood and getting her back on her feet. She was groggy but coming round, and, typical Nan, seemed more worried about all the fuss people were making than her injuries.

That's when I heard him – some 18- or 19-year-old in a blue

parka laughing his head off at my nan. I thought, "What the fuck? She's an old woman, you prick." Without thinking, I ran towards him and lashed out with my right fist. SMACK! And down he went with claret everywhere.

"Fucking laugh at my nan, you twat," I shouted. "Get up. Fucking get up."

But someone grabbed my arm and pulled me away before I could give him another shot. The lad stood up and, even though he was bigger than me, clearly didn't want to know, so he just staggered away while wiping the blood off his face.

I picked Nan up and we struggled on to the No. 3 bus. Just like always she was not worried about herself, only concerned I got into a fight and could have got hurt. It was only then I realised what I did – I was 13 but had laid out a grown man, leaving him screaming like a baby. It was a bit like it was the most important lesson of my life. If you're going to take someone on, get in first. In the years to come, running a pub, chasing down debts and dealing with some scary people, being able to look after myself was going to be a lifesaver.

Now you might suspect I threw this punch because, as a teenage Scouser, I was a complete knob, used to getting into fights all the time. Far from it. I can only remember a few occasions when I may have crossed the line, certainly in my primary school days. I was a good, honest kid.

Take school for example. I was never the greatest academic, but I did the homework and scraped through the exams. My first school, St Anthony's Catholic Primary, lives in my memory for mainly one thing. We've all read over the years about those dirty priests who liked to get off by molesting kids – well St Anthony's had its own questionable practices.

Occasionally, when the teacher decided you'd gone a bit too far in class or the playground, you were sent off to see one of the local priests who had the happy task of dishing out the discipline. What was wrong with detention or writing lines?

I can remember the priests' names, but I'll save their blushes. Let's just say given how we look at things today, Jimmy Savile and all that, they may be thinking they'll have a lot to answer for when they go upstairs to meet the Big Man. I'm not saying I was buggered or anyone else, but what happened wasn't right by any means. Whenever I was sent to see the priest, I knew what was coming. He'd call me into his office, cross hanging down from his neck and a stern look on his face.

First order of business was trousers and pants off. Then he put me across his knees and, with his bare hand, smacked my arse. Now where in the fucking Bible does Jesus tell his followers this is what they should be doing to young boys? And I guess they don't teach it at priest school, either.

After a good half dozen smacks – it hurt more if he hit you just at the top of your leg – he'd have enough and tell me to put my clothes back on.

"Ten Hail Marys and an Our Father and then come straight back," he'd say. Arse smarting, I'd go and kneel in the church begging God's forgiveness for whatever mortal sin I'd done. At the same time, I knew things with the priest weren't quite over. Before returning to school you went back to the priest for a final lesson. "Pants down," he'd shout before bending me across his knee to gently rub my still stinging backside.

Took me a long time to get over stuff like this, if I ever have. I don't know what it is with the Catholic Church, but you read about this and much worse all the time. I've never mentioned this to anyone before, but I suspect there are dozens of lads from St Anthony's who went through the same thing. I really do hope there's a Hell for those priests who were really abusive of the children they were supposed to look after. Fucking perverts.

One of the times that saw me sent off to the priest was after a run-in with a lad called Wrighty. He was the classic playground bully, who always picked on people who couldn't stand up for themselves. He would pick on someone different every day and just humiliate them. I knew one day it would be my turn. I wasn't afraid 'cos Dad had built a boxing ring in the garden so I fancied my chances of putting Wrighty in his place. As I would find out, though, it's a world of difference boxing away with your brothers with gloves on to standing toe to toe with just your bare fists.

One lunchtime in the playground, Wrighty decided he was going to put me in my place. I was a cocky little thing and up for it as soon as he had a go.

"Fight, fight, fight," one of the kids screamed and suddenly there were dozens around us as Wrighty and I started trading punches. You'd have thought I was some profession boxer dancing away like fucking Muhammad Ali, Queensberry rules and all that. Wrighty was taken a bit by surprise 'cos this ain't normally what happened. His victims never usually put up a fight.

After a couple of minutes, we were pretty evenly matched so that's when he started to play dirty. As I was swinging away, he suddenly grabbed hold of my hair and forced my head down, so I couldn't punch properly. Then, out of nowhere, he landed this punch straight on me head. BANG! I'm out cold. One of my mates tried to help out by launching himself at Wrighty, trying to hit him with a toy fire engine, but he only suffered the same fate. Thankfully it pretty much ended there when a couple of teachers appeared and sent everyone back to class – me, my mate and Wrighty were all sent straight off to see the priest to be lectured on the evils of fighting!

Somehow my dad had heard about the fight down at the fruit market where he worked. Dad's a straightforward type of guy – he wasn't happy I'd been fighting but he did his homework and was glad I'd only been sticking up for myself. His fatherly advice was just what I needed.

"Get him back tomorrow or his bullying will never end," he said. "Make sure you do it."

Cheers Dad, I thought. My head was still stinging from the day's beating and now you wanted me to do it all over again! Have to say it was a pretty restless night 'cos Wrighty had been quite a handful. If I were going to beat him, I'd have to play as dirty as him.

God smiles on the brave, they say – well he did the next morning as soon as I walked into school for morning assembly. All the kids were lined up, class by class, and there were teachers all over the place. Wrighty was grinning, probably looking forward to playtime when he could pick on me again. I thought, "Fuck him", pulled me arm back and then SMACK – punched him right in the face in front of the head, the teachers, everyone. Wrighty was lying on the floor, crying like a fucking baby. I knew he wouldn't bother me again. I knew there'd be shit to pay and, sure enough, went off to see the priest again before I had my first lesson. The school wrote to me parents but they didn't fuss. Wrighty was a bully, the school hadn't dealt with it, I had and they were proud I'd stood up for meself.

St Anthony's was followed by Lambeth Road Secondary Modern, right opposite our house and where my eldest brother,

Tony, was already a pupil along with a thousand other young Scousers. Tony's a sound lad, worked hard and had nowhere near as much trouble at primary as I'd had at St Anthony's.

Only two girls and one lad from St Anthony's had come with me to my new school so I knew virtually nobody. After my run in with Wrighty, I was a bit of a star, popular with everyone except the teachers. Arriving at Lambeth Road I was no longer going to be the immediate centre of attention, which bothered me. I suppose it's an adolescent thing because your mind is not thinking straight. I wanted to be "known", to be the fun guy everyone wanted to hang around with, to be a name! It wasn't going to be by being a swot and getting good grades. Weirdly for a Scouser, sport never interested me and that's surprising considering the whole fucking city lives and breathes football – Anfield and Goodison were both a stone's throw from our house.

So my dilemma was: how do I get everyone's attention? What was I really good at? What did I stand out for? I know, I thought, I'll play up with the teachers, that always works and this time there's no priest to be sent to. It seemed funny at the time but looking back it was fucking insane.

It was childish stuff at first – pins in chairs, ripping curtains, fucking around in the science labs. Pretty soon I was on every teacher's radar – when they saw me entering class, they'd all take a deep sigh knowing the next hour or so wasn't going to be easy. For them I was a complete pain in the arse, pretty apt really 'cos I saw more of the headmaster's office to be given the cane than I did the inside of a classroom. The head, Mr Patterson, and I were not friends.

It must be something about school assembly 'cos that's when the bubble really burst and I stepped up to the big time. Every

Friday the whole school would gather at 9am for the head to give his weekly address. We'd have to sit there as he'd drone on about new school rules or sporting and academic triumphs. I couldn't wait to get back to class and have some fun.

Anyway, on this one Friday morning there was something different planned for the assembly that the head knew would entertain the whole school.

On the stage stood Patterson and his arsehole deputy, Mr Whitby. I'm not listening to what's going on until one of me mates shoves me awake. Patterson was on the school stage calling my name.

"Shaun Smith! Shaun Smith!" he said. "Ah, there you are. Nice of you to join us this morning. Would you like to come up on stage please?"

One million per cent I was convinced I was about to get the cane in front of the whole school so it was with some nervousness I walked through the hall. I could hear everyone whispering as I made my way up. They all knew I was in the shit.

Patterson was standing there as I walked on to the stage, thankfully no cane in sight. What the fuck was going on?

"Shaun, could you just let the school know where you live?" he said. "In fact, no. Everybody, if you look through that window, you can see Shaun's house right there."

I should have mentioned that living directly opposite the school meant getting in on time was a problem, especially on the odd occasion when my dog, Shep, followed me in and I had to nip home with him and lock him indoors. I'd be reported for being late every other day by the teachers, who monitored the pupils arriving every morning.

Anyhow, everyone was still as confused as I was, wondering what Patterson was up to, when Whitby came forward and handed the prick what looked like a wooden clock.

"Here Shaun, we've specially made this for you in woodwork," he said. "You'll see we've set the time at 9.20am just for you, as that's the time you get here every bloody day."

At which point he hang the fucking thing round my neck and the whole hall laughed their fucking heads off. The cheeky, piss-taking bastards! If there's one thing I hate, it's someone taking the piss out of me. You'll see later on this is a bad mistake. It certainly was for those wankers Patterson and Whitby.

I wanted to smash that fucking clock right into Patterson's face but they sent me off the stage. Ha, ha, what a fucking hoot! If they tried that sort of thing with a pupil today they'd be all over the fucking papers. Not back in the '80s, though, as you could get away with that sort of thing. By the time I'd got to the first lesson, I was already planning my revenge. They'd made a laughing stock out of the wrong guy.

Like most young lads I had a paper round in the morning, which got me out of bed early. Usually, I'd be home pretty smartish, have a bit of brekkie and doss around for a bit before going over to school, always a bit late. The first couple of weeks after my public humiliation, though, I was a model pupil – to a degree. As soon as my round was finished I didn't bother going home but went straight over to school and quietly sneaked into the assembly hall. The stage where Patterson and Whitby hung that fucking clock round my neck was raised and on one side were two small doors that led to the storage area underneath holding old chairs and bits of scenery from school plays. Just the sort of stuff that should be thrown on a bonfire – which is exactly what I was planning.

Every time I crept under the stage I took old newspapers with me, stuffing them all over the place ready for my own Bonfire

Night, or, in this case, Bonfire Morning. It took me two weeks to get enough paper down there to make sure it would all go as planned.

Friday assembly finally arrived and, half an hour before it started, I crept into school and headed to the stage. I could hear the teachers above me, dragging chairs into place. Shit, I'm going to have to be careful here, I thought. If they don't fuck off out of the hall, they'll see me. Should I call it off? I'm just about to pack it in when the teachers leave and I get my chance. Lighter in hand I set my first bit of paper alight and scrambled to the doors, praying to God I don't go up with the inferno I was planning.

I ran straight down the hall and into the corridor and almost bumped into the French teacher, Mr Hunter. He had his head down in some books so I just slowed down and walked past him, praying he hadn't seen where I came from. For some reason, he ignored me and walked on by, allowing me to escape into the playground, which was already full of kids waiting for the bell to ring calling them to assembly.

Sure enough a few minutes later the bell sounded and we all piled in, with Patterson and Whitby at the centre of the stage as usual. All I could think of was the fire raging below.

We were called to silence as Patterson got to his feet and started talking but, as he did so, he and everyone else in the room suddenly smelt smoke and heard crackling. I thought "Fucking Scooby Doo" and mouth to my mates, "watch this".

Patterson called the caretaker over and as he went to the side of the stage to open the door – WOOSH – the rush of air going under the stage gave my bonfire all it needed to really get going.

"Fire, fire," screamed Patterson. "Everyone out, out!"

Inside I was pissing myself – make a fool out of me, you prick.

A few minutes later we were all lined up in the yard, like a roll call at a prisoner of war camp, while the fire brigade arrived to put the blaze out. We were standing there for what seemed ages when Whitby appeared and, surprise, surprise, guess whose name he called out?

"Shaun Smith, could you please go up to Mr Patterson's office," he belted out.

Game over. Hunter must have spotted me after all and put two and two together. I'm fucked. Just before I walked off to see Patterson, I remember I still had me Swan Vesta matches in my pocket, so quickly slipped them to me mate, Titch.

By the time I walked into Patterson's office, two policemen – my first encounter with the bizzies – were sitting by his desk. They didn't look very friendly.

Patterson didn't hang about. "Smith, stand there, hands behind your back," he said. "You know what's happened. We believe you started this fire. This is very serious, Smith. What have you got to say?"

"No way, sir, no way," I protested. "I was in assembly like everyone else when it kicked off. How could it be me?"

"Mr Hunter saw you, Smith."

"Oh, I knew you'd bring that up. Couple of weeks ago when you made me look like a prat in front of the whole school I dropped my special pen onstage. I've been looking for it ever since and was under there searching, that's all. If I set it on fire how come it wasn't all burning when we all came in? I knew you'd pick on me – I want Mum and Dad here 'cos this ain't fair. You shouldn't be talking to me without me parents here; I know that much."

So they called home and Mum was in and over she came. She wasn't happy and, like them, could see straight through my story. But she wasn't going to let them know that, instead doing exactly as I knew she would and defending me to the hilt. Three days suspension.

It was the day to go back and Dad decided to come with me to see Patterson together. First, though, I was left outside his office staring at the school trophy cabinet as the two of them discussed my woeful performance and future. Eventually, I was summoned in and Dad looked furious, learning about all the stuff I was getting up to for the first time.

"Stand up straight, Smith," Patterson said. "I just want to say in all my years of being a teacher and a headmaster I have never ever felt like punching a pupil in the face but I want to do that to you, Smith."

Imagine – he wanted to fucking punch me. Come on Dad, this ain't right, I thought.

"Don't you worry Mr Patterson," said Dad. "Wait 'til I get him home. Shit, the bizzies weren't half as scary as what's coming."

As it turns out, though, Dad never raised his hand when I got in but I knew both he and Ma were seriously pissed off with me.

Patterson, though, still wasn't finished with me. After the Friday meeting with me dad, I turned up Monday and immediately I was called to his office. This time the cane was out and he was ready. WHACK. Finally, it was over and I couldn't resist it.

"Are you finished yet?" I said. "How many did you give me? Six?"

I was not letting him know it fucking hurt like shit. He was livid but couldn't do any more. Wanker.

School was a disaster after this. The few teachers I did get on with soon became twats like everyone else and what little interest I had left soon vanished and further suspensions followed. Opening all the radiator valves in an upper floor corridor didn't go down too well, I remember. They tried to get me moved to another school but nobody wanted the grief that was certain to come with me. So I stayed, the teachers hated me and I hated them. Eventually, I decided there was only one thing to do – I'd burn the whole place down, but this time it would work.

It was the same plan as before, only slightly modified. I put papers under the stage, but this time I would make sure they'd burn a lot faster by soaking them in lighter fuel. Bloody idiot – I was too clever by half.

When the day came, I crept into school half an hour before assembly to give my fire time to get going. I was back under the stage, but when I took my lighter out to set fire to the first bits of paper – WHOOSH. It was like a fucking flamethrower with the fuel-soaked paper all over the place catching light. Fuck! Get out quick, I thought, before the whole place goes up. Back through the assembly hall and the fire alarms were going before I was even back in the yard. I didn't even bother to stop, just legged it straight through the gates and dashed over the street to home. I took the morning off and went in at lunchtime.

Within seconds of walking into school, I was spotted by one of the teachers and dragged off to see Patterson. He was not hanging about this time. He was straight on the phone to Mum and Dad, and we all went off to the police station.

I pleaded my innocence, saying I was just skiving, but inside I was pissing myself because by now the kids were all sent home. It was a proper fire, good job. That's when Mum, my hero, got serious.

"Don't look to us for help, son," she said. "This is getting serious now. Just think what this is doing to your dad and me and the family. Do you want a criminal record?"

But I wasn't listening, by then I wasn't arsed by anything, though looking back I should have been.

Amazingly the bizzies only gave me a caution. Should have got a lot more, considering.

Another thing was that I was finally out of Lambeth Street. Patterson wouldn't have me back so I was shipped off to Penguin Street School – just for people like me, trouble – with the delightful Mr Cartwright in charge. He was the biggest prick of them all.

First day, Cartwright calls me in for a chat. He'd done his homework and got straight to the point.

"Smith, this is not your normal school," he said. "What I say goes. I'm not a normal teacher, and I won't put up with any of your shit."

Fair enough, he's made his case, so a couple of days later I decide to set out my own stall. Every day, Cartwright came to school on an old Lambretta mod scooter, with mirrors everywhere, that he kept padlocked at the front of the building. I can have a bit of fun with that, I thought, liven up the morning for everyone.

I was able to break the lock with just a pair of scissors, so I kick-started the engine and raced around the school corridors, hitting cupboards, walls and doors. It sent his mirrors flying off everywhere.

Oh, I forgot to mention I'd also sneaked into Cartwright's office and put sherbert in his aquarium. He liked his fish but they didn't like the sherbert.

This time there was murder to pay. Mum was called in straightaway and there was only one outcome. Cartwright didn't hang about and gave me a straight red – I was expelled.

Dad lost the plot.

"Do you know how hard me and your mum work?" he screamed. "Fuck up again and bring shame to this family then watch what you get from me – that's a promise."

He kept his cool right up until I had a spot of bother with a local lad, known to everyone as Mongy Pete as he was a bit short upstairs, if you follow my drift. Usually Mongy Pete was alright, always happy and smiling, wouldn't say boo to a goose. But then this one day out of the blue he turned up at ours and nicked me brother's bike.

As soon as I found out, I tracked him down and, after a few slaps, recovered the bike. Dad just happened to pull right at this moment and as soon as he saw him, Mongy Pete screamed, "He hit me, he hit me." Now what I didn't know was Pete was on some pretty heavy medication and he'd missed taking it that day, which is why he'd somehow got it in his head to waltz off with our Brendan's bike. Dad took in the scene and all he could see is me – the bad lad – having slapped this poor lad who really couldn't hurt a fly. Dad was spot on and it was all he needed to finally make up for holding his hand on all my other shit. He dragged me indoors and then off he went, Doc Martens landing all over me, slapping and punching, all the time Mum and me sister are screaming at him to stop. There's no way I'd ever try and hit back so I was just covering up as best I could thinking "fucking twat" when he suddenly stopped and left the room.

"Bloody twat fuck the lot of yez," I shouted thinking it was over but then he came back. He had only gone and changed his boots, putting his steelies on before getting back to work. Two broken ribs followed before Mum could get him off.

Dad stood there at the end and, dead cold, spelled it out: "I am telling you now that's the last time. Next time I'll kill you."

I screamed back at him as he walked away, but in truth I was scared.

It took some time before it dawned on me I shouldn't be putting my parents through shit like this. They always worked hard and did their best for me so why should they suffer for the stuff I got up to?

Simple, I won't tell them what's happening in my life. What they don't know can't hurt them.

That's why I got so pissed off with a prick called Mr Conlon, the miserable old one-legged geezer who was one of the customers on my paper round.

My shift took in four 22-storey blocks, and my dogs Shep and Sam were always with me running up the stairs as the lifts fucking never worked.

I hated doing Conlon as he was always such a twat. I'd knock his door and there he'd be sitting in front of the telly, his false leg lying against the back of his chair.

One afternoon I walked in shouting, "Are you there Mr Conlon?"

"Is that you Shaun?" he said. "Come here lad. Could you do me a favour and run down to the Pacific to get me a couple of bottles of Guinness?"

Fuck, this was a pain in the arse as he was the last delivery on the round and I'd have to wait around the pub 'til someone would go in and buy the beers for me 'cos I was still well under age to get served.

Reluctantly I took his money, headed down to the pub, finally got the beers and headed back to his flat. He was watching the box as I gave him his Guinness and put the change by the telly. Job done, and off I went with not a word of thanks from the miserable old sod.

Next morning I was there again delivering his News of the World when, out of the blue, he suddenly kicked off.

"Come here you little thief, where's my money?" he shouted. "I'm going to tell your dad you stole it from me. He'll fucking kill you."

I tried to fight my corner, telling him where I'd put his change the night before, but he wasn't having any of it. Fuck, I thought, that's the last thing I need, more grief for Dad. He'll go fucking mad if he thinks I've now started thieving on top of everything else.

Lucky for me, though, Conlon rarely went out and it never got back to Dad. I was worried for days that it would all kick off, but when it hadn't by the end of the week I knew I was all right. Time for a bit of fun with Conlon for putting me through this grief.

Saturday afternoon he would be expecting the sports paper, The Pink. I knew he always kept his door open and, with any luck, after his usual half dozen bottles of beer, he'd be fast asleep in his chair. My luck was in as, when I crept into his flat, I could hear him snoring like a drunken pig. I wasn't sure exactly what I was planning to do but then God smiled on me – the prick's artificial leg was there lying on the back of his chair. I slid across the floor, folded it into my newspaper sack and crept from the flat leaving Conlon stranded.

The leg came in handy when I was on my way home shortly afterwards. I met some of my mates who were playing penalties and said, "Here lads, bet the lot of yers I can score without using me legs or me head."

Down went their cash. Not a lot but a couple of quid at least.

The keeper was standing there ready when I pulled Conlon's leg out of me bag and smacked the ball straight past him.

I thought, "I wonder if I can do something like this again?"

CHAPTER 2
THE NEWSAGENT

There's been many parts of my life, some good, some bad, but that's the way the cards fell and I've just got on with it. Mine has been the sort of life you don't see on telly, and you couldn't imagine the things I've seen and done. Always, though, I've been able to make my way by remembering those early lessons – get in first and don't ever let anyone take the piss. It's why people have always come to me for help because they know I can get things sorted. Today, when someone in my world runs into trouble, when someone owes them or if they have nowhere else to turn, that's where I step in. There are no solicitors here with legal letters flying around with fuck all ever being achieved. If someone knocks my door, the debt owed to them becomes my debt. The fucker who won't pay up won't know anything until I knock on his door.

The first time I remember playing the collector was for a lad called Frank. He worked hard part-time for a minibus company, but for six months they bounced him for £2,600 and there was no way he could get them to pay up.

I explained the terms for Frank – no money up front as the debt is small but whatever I recover I take 35 per cent. Done.

So off I trotted to see the bloke who owned the bus company, let's call him Dave, expecting this to be a simple job. Wrong. I got to the van yard, walked into the office and asked for Dave, who is one cheeky fucker. He just couldn't understand that the money he owed Frank now had to be paid to me and got very lippy, threatening the bizzies and all that crap. But I got his attention so there was no need for anything to kick off. I made my excuses and said I would be back at noon on Friday. And, as a bit of advice, I told him to do his homework on me.

Friday arrived. I got there an hour early and walked straight into his office and he immediately started bleating that times were hard and he couldn't pay. He offered £100 a week but, fuck that, I wasn't waiting six months for me money. I looked out of his office and there were buses all over the yard coming and going so he was obviously doing well. Bad mistake because he was taking the piss. Simple solution, I thought, he can pay in kind, so I left the office and jumped on the first bus I saw parked outside. It was probably no different to driving a car, I thought. Not a chance! This thing wasn't going anywhere and I couldn't even find out how to close the door. There's another problem, too – the fucking thing hadn't moved for months and wasn't going anywhere. By this time there were mechanics appearing from everywhere and heading my way with Dave leading the charge.

"If you want the bus you can fucking have it you prick," he shouted. "I'll just report it stolen and get paid out on the insurance."

What do you do? Stuck in the bus on me own, I'm going nowhere.

"Let's have a cup of tea and sort it," I suggested.

Ten minutes later it was agreed – he paid £1,200 up front and by the following Friday he had done his homework and paid the rest. I learned a few good lessons, though – it's a bad idea to go alone as it could have got quite tasty. And never get on a bus.

In this game you never know who's going to ask for your help. I was in my pub one Sunday morning – I ran one for years – when in walked this Pakistani fella who ran a corner shop. All I've ever said to him is "20 Woodbines and an Echo" so I'm a bit surprised to see him in the bar asking for a chat.

Off he started on some boring shite about how he bought

his cousin over from Pakistan and set him up in a shop just a few doors down from his own, but gave him one condition – he couldn't sell ciggies or booze. So guess what the reward was for all his good efforts? The minute his cousin opened his store he went straight into direct competition with his cousin.

That's when he got to the point.

"What I would like Shaun is for you to shoot him in the foot," he said. "In my culture, if he has a bad foot everyone will know he's a bad man and turn their backs on him. For this I will pay you £3,500."

Now as you can imagine, I'm not averse to the odd pound note, but this guy had seriously got things arse about tit. But if he had some money to throw around, I was happy to discuss it. With the pub busy, I sent him off and agreed to meet him a few days later at his flat above his shop.

When I popped round later, he was sat on the sofa, wife by his side and the first thing he handed me was a pistol, which was probably 100 years old, and one bullet. He even got me a balaclava and a pair of Marigolds. And the cash was there. Happy days.

"Listen," I explained. " I can sort this without having to shoot anyone. Just give me the cash and I'll take care of it."

I couldn't get out the place fast enough with the couple shouting, "Good luck Shaun, good luck!"

It took him a couple of weeks to work it out and finally he came into the pub one Monday morning.

"You bloody thief. You took my money and did nothing," he shouted. "My cousin still has good feet."

"What are you going to do, dickhead?" I said. "Call the bizzies? Don't be a twat. When you came in here asking me to shoot your cousin, I got it all on the pub's CCTV so you're fucked. Who's going down for that? You, you prick, so just fuck off."

I shopped at his cousin's after that.

Now you're probably starting to see that in my game you never know how things are going to turn out. Life's full of surprises. Take my mate Copoff. He's a nice fella. He's a roofer who we met in a restaurant in Deansgate in Manchester. It was a posh Italian place full of wannabes. Strange name, Copoff, but given the number of women he picked up not hard to imagine why. We hadn't seen him for a few months then, out of the blue, I got a phone call inviting me to his wedding. Given his form you just knew it wouldn't last.

So we trotted off to the wedding and it was a big, big do that must have cost thousands. That was the last I heard from him, but no worries, we had a good time.

Two years later, I'm in my office when the phone goes. It's another job. This time the client was a small-time scaffolder who was owed £17,000, which, in his world, is a lot of money. In my world, too, especially as I would be nicking 35 per cent.

The debtor was a bloke called Kevin, who runs a roofing company in Stoke. It's not too far to travel, so the next day I shot off down the M6 and parked up outside his yard and rang his office number.

"Hello, is Kevin there please?" I said. "No, okay could you ask him to ring me? My name is Shaun Smith and I need to speak to him urgently."

I hung up and a few minutes later me phone went and Kevin was on the line.

"I thought you weren't in, mate?" I said. "Your office number has come up on my phone, you prick. And if you look out the window you can see me."

I start waving from the yard.

So he came out and invited me in for a chat. I explained the situation and that's when he played his card – he was not the owner of the business, just the manager. Some bloke called Gary was the boss and held all the money.

"I don't give a fuck mate," I said. "I'll be back Friday and there better be some money."

Two days later I'm back and there was progress – £3,700 handed straight over and the promise to pay Frank the remainder at £1,000 a week. Job done, I thought, and I would sort out my bit with Frank after he got sorted.

A month goes by and then Frank was back on the phone. They stopped paying him and those Stoke fuckers can't be found. Frank was so fed up he handed the whole lot over to me because he just wanted to walk away. There was nine grand left on the table. Game on!

Now in my game, if you really want to make a point there's no better way than to call up some reserves – in this case 15 of my traveller mates. They're quite partial to a flat back truck and it was in two of these they drove into the roofer's yard the following Friday afternoon. As Cilla, God rest her soul, would say, "surprise surprise" and within seconds my mobile rang.

"Is that you, Shaun?" the bloke said. "This is Gary in Stoke."

But there was something wrong. The number he rang from was already in my contacts. It was fucking COPOFF. It was me mate!

"Shaun," he shot down the phone. "I need fucking help.

There's a load of travellers in me yard ready to kick off. Do you know anyone who can sort it?"

I cannot fucking believe it.

"Copoff, do me a favour will ya? Just shout out Johnnie and see if you can get him to the phone."

I quickly explained the situation to Johnnie, but told him not to let on that they were all there working for me. There was a chance to save a few bob as Johnnie and his mates were still going to need paying for their time and services. It's a long drive from Manchester to Stoke after all. I got Copoff back on the phone and he quickly agreed to hand over two grand to Johnnie and his mates, who head off to the pub.

Next week Copoff and I met up in that posh Italian, San Lorenzo, in Manchester, and the champagne started flowing.

"Thank God for your help last week mate," he said. "Without you I'd be screwed."

Now at this point I'm still nine big pound notes out of pocket, but Kevin slipped an envelope across the table and inside there is £10,000.

"Seriously mate, I think I'd be dead without you," he said.

And the marriage? He lived up to his nickname. She caught him playing away a few months after the wedding.

CHAPTER 3
THE FOOTBALL MANAGER

There's a guy I know, Bill, who, now and then, puts a decent job my way. He's a great bloke and straight-up fella. He knows he can trust me one million per cent 'cos I'll do a job right, no matter how tricky it looks.

Back in December 2014, he gave me a bell at this nice little gym I own. He had another great job for me – a Premier League football manager has come to Bill for help. Let's call him Eamon Kelly to save his blushes but you all know him. Funny bloke, on the telly all the time.

Anyway turns out Eamon's got a lad, Joe, who's a total wanker. Cost his dad a couple of million bailing him out of the shit. Businesses, credit cards, bank loans, the lot. Way, way too late, Eamon pulled down the shutters at the Bank of Dad and told Joe to fuck off and stand on his own two feet.

Easier said than done when you haven't got a fucking clue about anything. Joe, though, thought he was the fucking bollocks and could do it all without his old man's help. He had got loads of business ideas, he thought, so all he needed was the money to get things off the ground. The problem is he had no chance of borrowing from any normal lenders given how piss poor his credit rating was.

Now Joe's probably fucked up a thousand times in his life but this time he excelled himself. Like a fucking idiot, he hooked up with some bad men in Manchester and borrowed £100,000 to get his plans up and running. Now these people aren't like the nice men in suits at Barclays – their interest rates come from La La Land and non-payment is not an option. If the lender can't pay, it can get very, very serious and we're not talking County Court here, more like A&E.

So 12 months in and, sure enough, Joe was in the shit. He had money coming in, but the interest on the loan is a fucking disaster – he handed over £200,000 already and now they were hitting him for another 87 large ones and he had nowhere to go.

So the lenders did what comes naturally to them. They don't care who pays so long as they get their money. If Joe can't pay up, they decide, let's go and knock on daddy's door. He's sure to pay up to save his lad getting in even worse bother than he already is.

Picture the scene: it was a typical Sunday morning and Eamon's lovely wife was stood in the kitchen of their luxury home, bacon sizzling and kettle whistling. Eamon was on the loo having a crap and reading the papers, checking yesterday's match reports. Fucking reporters, he thought, what fucking game were they watching?

Back in the kitchen, his wife was about to take the bacon out from under the grill when suddenly she looked round and there, inside the doorway, were two of the biggest black guys she had ever seen.

"Where's Joe?" they said. "Where is he? We want our money. Get him to pay or get his dad to pay. Just get it fucking sorted."

She was fucking shitting herself and screamed loud enough to wake the dead. Eamon desperately tried to get out of the crapper to find out what was going on but, by the time he got to the kitchen, the two guys left. They were just there to deliver a message, that's all. A bit heavy handed, but, job done, there was no need to hang around so they were on their toes pretty sharpish.

Eamon had a simple choice here – ring the bizzies or try and sort it himself. Now, if you know anything about Eamon, he's quite a private guy and not much of one for the authorities. Likes to play by his own rules. He got in a few scrapes every now and again, but always sorted it. Lucky fella, to be honest.

After he calmed the missus down, he rang Joe to find out what the fuck this was all about and then he found out his lad had done it again and landed him straight into the shitter. Same as before, Eamon could let Joe sort it himself or step in. If he called the police it would leak out, as someone's always going to be ringing the papers tipping them off for a few quid.

Eamon was smart enough to know his son was way out of his depth, but he knew that, like any business, there was a way to sort this without it ending in tears. He sailed close to the wind several times himself, so Eamon knew a few people on the fringes of the world his "visitors" came from. There was bound to be someone who could help.

So he rang a friend, who rang a friend who rang Billy who rang me. I rang Eamon.

Just 24 hours later, I was sat in front of him in his amazing fucking house. He was pretty shaken by yesterday's events and was desperate for the whole thing to go away as quickly as possible. Don't worry, I told him, I would handle everything. There'll be no-one at his house again, and it'll all stay private. My job was to get the lenders to agree a settlement, which wouldn't be easy, but I was confident I could get a deal. For that I wanted £10k upfront and half of any amount I end up saving him. If you don't like it this way, I told him, you can find someone else but you won't get a better deal and there are very few people around who you could go to.

I could see he didn't like it but we shook on it. I'm sure he was more pissed off with Joe for getting him in this crap than the idea of having to pay me to sort it.

As it happened, of course, the sort of people Joe dealt with move in a very small world and it was just my luck that I had known the lender for years. He is a very serious player, into all sorts of things. He was also absolutely the last fucking person on the planet Joe should ever have got involved with. If I'm going to sort this stuff out, I thought, I would have to be right on me game.

First off I tracked down the lender and, from the start, he was not overly happy that I was now involved. It was easy for him chasing little Joe but an entirely different story now he had to talk to me. But money talks and, if he was going to get any, he knew it would be going through me now.

On Christmas Eve we agreed to meet at the Lowry Hotel in Manchester. It was a bit grand for what's about to be played out but, hey ho.

I arrived early taking Billy and me mate Tiny – think Little John – who may not be the sharpest tool in the box but is very handy to have around. I also stuck another lad, Andy, in the car park. It's always good to have a reserve if needed. He was sat outside in my Merc watching as the lender turned up in his new Range Rover with blacked-out windows. Andy watched the Rover park up and then called me so I knew he was on the way up to the room. Billy knew what was going down but Tiny didn't have a clue. He guessed he was just there to provide a bit of muscle.

"Do you want me to knock him out as soon as he comes in Shaun?" asked Tiny.

"Do I fuck!" I said. "Do you want to cause World War Three? When he knocks, just let him come in, you fucking idiot. If I need you to do anything, I'll fucking tell ya."

The door knocks and Tiny walked over to let the lender in.

"Hiya mate," he said, playing it dead cool. He sat straight down and put his phones on the table: one, two, three, four, five, six of the fuckers.

"You can put them away for a fucking start," I said. "Which one's got the recorder running?"

"Don't panic mate, these are me work phones," said the lender. "You think I'm going to sit here talking about Eamon Kelly with me phones running? Don't be a prick."

Good point, he'd fit himself up. Stay calm.

"Oh come on Shaun," said the lender. "Forget the phones. Let's just agree how we get some fucking money off this twat. He's a fucking millionaire for Christ's sake. His lad's been paying so they'll pay more. Come on – I've already done him a favour and knocked it down from £100k to £87k."

"Yes," I asked, "but where did that fucking number come from? Why not 85 or 88?"

"Compound interest."

"For fuck's sake, you don't even know what that means let alone how to fucking work it out."

And then Billy piped up.

"It's not happening, never," he said. "No way you're getting that sort of money."

"You can shut the fuck up mate," said the lender. "Who the fuck are you anyway? You're not in our circle. Shaun and I will sort this, so fuck off. Now come on Shaun, we can both make a few quid from this. Just tell them how bad I am, what sort of things I can do to him."

"I know what you can do but not now," I said. "You've already milked this fucking big time. We need to make a deal and end it. I am looking at the bigger picture here."

The bigger picture I had was that if I did a good job for Eamon Kelly, he would owe me big time, maybe enough to put my name around in his world. There's bound to be a tonne of shit going on with other managers and players. Shit that I could sort out. With the money floating around in the Premier League, it would be big, big paydays.

Now as this went on, this lad's phone kept ringing and he made out that he was doing business with a big firm. But I had seen all these games before, it was probably one of his lads sitting out in the car who was told to ring the phones every couple of minutes.

The lender was not thinking about the future, though, just the money he was chasing right now.

"Let's cut the bullshit," I said. "You are not getting £87,000."

He wouldn't be here if he wasn't prepared to cut a deal, so I knew he had a number in mind that he would settle on.

"What do you think he will go for," he answered, "£50k? 'Cos I'm not budging below that, no fucking way."

I could take that back to Eamon, but I don't want the lender to know I'm ready to settle. I had to make it look like he was breaking my balls.

"Fuck off £50,000, no way," I said. "Fuck it, if I have to fall out with you, I'll fall out with you. But I'll tell you what I will do. I'll put two lads outside Eamon Kelly's house 'cos you ain't getting to him. And if you want to go to his business, go ahead and see what happens. The bizzies will be on you as fast as flies on shit. Threatening a Premier League manager, get real. That's why you need to listen to me. You can forget your compound interest shit. You've already had £100k for fuck's sake. Whatever you get now is a bonus."

"I ain't going below £50k. Not a chance."

"I hear ya so here's what I'll do. I will go and tell Eamon you want £50,000, and we'll see what he says. Whatever it is, I will see you on New Year's Day, good or bad, and we can take it from there. If you and I are going to fall out over it, okay, but we'll keep it on the streets, no family."

"Okay, Shaun. Let's try it your way."

So the next day I'm on the phone to Eamon Kelly.

"I'm not paying it. Why should I?" he said. "My son's already given them a fortune."

"Eamon, I am not being funny, but you can afford £50,000. You spend that on a fucking weekend away with your bird or on a yacht. Fifty fucking grand, you probably lose that on a weekend's betting. It's nothing to you. Go and fucking sign someone's T-shirt or get someone to sponsor you. You'll get it back."

But he didn't budge so the call ended. I tried again on New Year's Eve 'cos the lender wanted an answer the next morning.

"Listen Eamon what is the most you can push to? I don't want to fall out with these people because they are a reputable firm, just pretty heavy. I just want to cut a deal and get on with my life. I'm in the business of making friends, not enemies. I've gone out on a limb here to sort this for you – and remember you asked for my help, I didn't come to you."

"But I don't want to pay, so why should I?" he said.

"Look, if these people give you a hard time, you are not going to like it, mate. They might not get to you but your wife is going to go shopping or you can send her on a cruise and you won't be there to watch her back. And Joe's still walking around, but who's looking after him? You don't want it, mate, just fucking pay them, however much it hurts."

"Okay, I'll pay £35,000. And how much do I pay you?"

It was fucking hard work getting him to pay anything, so I didn't want to fuck this up by playing hardball for myself. I was generous and knocked off the percentage he originally agreed he'd pay from any amount I'd saved him. With the original debt at £87,000 and him settling at £35,000, I said goodbye to 26 fucking grand.

"Call it £10,000 and we're done."

"Great, get me their account number and I'll transfer the money."

Next thing I'm sitting down with the lender and he went through the motions of kicking off but eventually calms down. He took the £35k but wanted to know what I was getting.

"Just a little tickle," I told him.

Okay, it should have been a big tickle but, with £10k and Eamon spreading my name around, there'll be bigger paydays to come.

As I said earlier, life is full of fucking surprises, and, guess what, now fucking Eamon took the piss.

A month on, the lender had his bill settled, but there was no sign of any money for me. I didn't want to fuck things up so I took it back to Billy who gave me the job in the first place. I'm sat there when Billy called him at his training ground. They were on the loudspeaker so I could hear every word. Billy gets straight down to business.

"Eamon, sorry to bother ya," he said. "Look, I've had Shaun on the phone and he says he's still waiting for the money you owe him. There's no problem, is there?"

"What money?" he shouted. "Fucking hell – have I got to pay that cunt as well? I've just paid 35 grand for my fucking son – he's just as bad as them."

He didn't know I was listening and Billy could see I was about to explode. I want to wring his fucking neck.

"Listen Eamon, you know what the deal was: £35,000 now and £10,000 for Shaun. You were paying 87 remember? Shaun's saved you plenty and you've got your life back. Your bird hasn't got to worry about people popping up in her garden. Is that not worth 10 grand?"

"I'm not fucking happy with this."

"But you had a deal with Shaun, Eamon."

"I had no deal with Shaun."

And with that the phone went down. Fucking piss-taking bastard. What did he think I was fucking doing all this time – fucking charity? Now clearly I was not happy but Billy promised to sort it 'cos at the end of the day he's the one who set the whole thing up.

Six months went by and fuck all happened. Billy ain't delivered so it was time to pay Eamon a visit. Into the Merc with me missus and a couple of mates and off we went. I wondered if he would invite us in for a cup of tea?

I knocked Eamon's door but there was no answer, so I popped over the wall and into his garden (beautiful house by the way, lovely views). He really should beef up his security – it was a piece of piss to break in.

One of the neighbours spotted me and threatened to call the police. I'm a registered debt collector so, as soon as I told them what I'm up to, delivering an invoice for services rendered, it wasn't going to take long 'til someone at the cop shop sold that juicy piece of gossip to the tabloids.

Sadly the police never came but someone had seen us and, the next minute, Eamon was on the phone to Billy telling him to get me away from his house or he would call the bizzies. So fucking what? Bring it on.

He was now taking the piss BIG TIME and wound me up so much that I thought he could fuck off for just 10 grand. If he said there was no deal at 10 for me and 35 for the lender, then we could go back to the original agreement we sat in his house and shook hands on.

I'm ready to go when Billy got back in touch. Eamon rang him back and filled him in on what's been going on. Turns out he had the massive hump with his son, Joe, and this latest episode was the final straw. All totalled he spent a million on him over five years – that's a lot of fatherly love. He told Billy any money I was owed was his son's problem, not his.

Now I've got Joe's number so make the call.

"How does a grand a week sound?" Joe suggested.

"How does fuck off sound?" I said. "I want me fucking money. Listen, people could have been hurt here. I put your life back together. This sounds like a clear message to me you're very scared of the people I fucked off. You paid them 'cos you're scared of them. Tell you what, let's see if you like this."

I hung up and rang Eamon's club.

"Is Eamon Kelly there please?" I said.

"Who's calling?" said the girl at the club.

"Shaun Smith. I've been working with him and his son, Joe."

"Sorry, Mr Kelly's not here at the moment. Can he call you back or email?"

"Sure just email me at ukdebtcollectors.com as quickly as possible. He needs to settle his account. I really don't want to have to come to the ground to serve papers on him in front of everyone because it just wouldn't look right. Thanks."

I could hear the secretary's chin hitting her desk – what a story!

A few minutes later, Billy got the call. Eamon was not happy. How dare I ring his office and try to embarrass him. Thankfully,

Billy ain't having any of it and told him plain and simple my money needed to be paid.

Next minute, Joe was on the phone to Billy and said he was putting money into my account. It wasn't the full amount, but, for the moment, I could let that ride. I could knock Eamon's door anytime and he knew it. Maybe I'll need a favour one day.

There's also another upside on this deal. Billy knew I was pissed off with him 'cos he brought the whole package to me and it had been nothing but a pain in the arse. He knew he needed to make it up.

As it happened, though, what a nice little earner that turned out to be.

CHAPTER 4
THE ROLEX

The jobs I really, really love are when big businesses rip off the little fella trying to make a few bob and end up dealing with me.

Billy knew he owed me one so he gifted me a beauty worth more than the money owed. A traveller called Mickey was taken on by one of the biggest construction firms in the North East. The company is worth millions and doesn't care who it fucks over. Mickey worked for them as a subcontractor for six years by which time the business owed him £86,000. A lot of money, but absolutely nothing to the big firm. Mickey's problem was letting his invoices pile up because, before he asked for payment, the directors "bumped" the company – that's when a business shuts down one day but then opens up soon after with all the same jobs and gear.

Nice for them but not for Mickey. The company's problem now, though, is it's me they now owe. So I went down to its offices with one of my lads and asked for one of the bosses, Steve, who I was told was a cocky, arrogant fat little fucker. And German, too. Spot on.

"Who the fuck are you? A fucking debt collector?" he asked.

"Listen, dickhead, I am not your average debt collector," I replied. "Here's me bill."

I handed him an invoice for £86k, but he started bleating that he didn't owe anyone and had never heard of Mickey.

"You don't owe him, you owe me and I'm a different kettle of fish," I explained. "Pay the money or get me someone to speak to who fucking can. You'll pay the money."

He was getting a bit nervous so to calm things down I left me number and told him to get someone to call me.

Surprise, surprise, a couple of days later the bizzies knocked the door but it was just for a quiet chat as they knew I was playing within the rules.

Fair enough, two can play at that game, so I tracked down gobby Steve's home address and paid him a visit to see how he likes it.

"Hiya, I'm Shaun Smith. Is your husband in?" I said.

"Sorry he's just gone, can I help?" his missus replied.

"Has he left that money? The 86 grand? He said he was leaving it today. It's a cash thing he owes someone."

"Who are you, Shaun Smith?"

Message delivered, I got back in the car. Steve was on the phone in seconds.

"Don't be knocking my door, bothering me bird," he shouted.

But the cheeky twat said he was still not paying.

Now I can see from his attitude this is going to be a long and difficult process and I was explaining this to Billy when he came up with a cracking idea. If they won't play ball then we should perhaps recover Mickey's money in kind. They're a huge company working on massive building projects and that means very big, very expensive machinery. The site Mickey was working on when they'd bumped the company had one of those machines that crush bricks and masonry, worth at least 40 grand. So we decided to have it away. Dead easy when you know how, especially as Mickey still had a key!

So we saddled up, and Mickey and I headed off to the site. There was a guard there but nothing to worry about as Mickey knew him for years. A £20 note let us in. Now what does he think we'll be doing next? Two lads late at night with a 40ft flat trailer?

The lad on the gate went off for a cuppa as Mickey got the key, climbed into the crusher and drove it up into the trailer.

With his yellow lights flashing, he drove out of the yard as I followed in me Merc to one of Mickey's mate's yards. Nice one.

So we had £40k in the bank but there was still some work to do.

Mickey found out there was another piece of gear, a massive digger, worth at least £90,000, which he was pointed to. In the building game, this is the sort of stuff you hire and pay about £1,500 a day, maybe needing it for a couple of weeks.

Steve's lot – and I can't blame 'em – hired this kit and then a couple of weeks later reported it stolen to the lenders. Truth is they had it away and were running it for months on other sites saving themselves a fortune. And guess what? We now knew where it was.

Mickey and I arrived at this farm at 10 o'clock and there, behind a barn, was this huge machine all loaded up on a trailer ready to go. Fuck it, let's take a chance, I thought. Who dares wins!

As we drove into the farm, this bloke suddenly appeared – gotta be someone Steve's lot put on his land to keep an eye on the gear.

"Hey, what you doing?" he shouted.

"None of your business mate, just fuck off will ye," I replied.

"No, this is my business."

"Fuck you mate, you know what's going on. We're taking that and if you behave you can have five grand, understand?"

Now he probably just got a drink for letting Steve stash the machine on the farm, so five grand is a touch. His loyalty to Steve went out the window.

"I'm not fucking arsed mate. I'll take five grand."

Then Mickey and I started hooking the trailer onto our rig when suddenly two other lads popped out of a caravan, the sort

44

you can tip up. I could see they wanted to be heroes.

"Hey what you doing? You won't be taking that – and I'll tell yez why, 'cos we've got the fucking key."

Fuck. Time for a chat. So Mickey and I walked over to the caravan and tried to reason with them.

"Listen lads the farmer's been paid five grand so leave it will ya," I said.

"What do ya mean the farmer's been paid five grand?" he replied.

"We've paid him five grand to take that."

"It's fuck all to do with him."

Oops but I'm not paying anyone else.

"Not my problem lads. You want some money, go and speak to him."

They were still banging on his door as we drove the rig out of the yard and off into the night.

The following week, Mickey had the £40k machine on a ferry over to Ireland and shipped the bigger gear down South where he hired it out for the day rate for the next six months 'til he made enough to cover the original debt. He followed that with a quick sale to a fellow traveller.

Steve, though, can't let it go and had the balls to call me.

"You cheeky bastard, you've robbed our gear," he said.

"Listen you prick, you'd already robbed one of these machines so shut the fuck up," I replied.

"How did you find that out?"

"It doesn't fucking matter mate, that's why I'm good at my job. You should have paid me but instead you took the piss. Big mistake."

Happy days.

There's been quite a few times when jobs I've taken on have worked out because the people I'm chasing know they're in the wrong and can't do anything about it. Like Steve.

Here's another example, a scrap metal dealer I know in Birmingham – we'll call him Steptoe for old time's sake. Him and his lad were out doing their rounds one day when they stumbled across an old working men's club which had been shut for years. As luck would have it, some dodgy developer had been looking round the place earlier in the day and one of his oppos was just locking up when Steptoe arrived.

He asked if there was any scrap inside he could take away for him and this lad, who we'll call Dave, thought he would be doing his boss a favour and invited Steptoe to fill his boots. Tables, chairs, old fridges – everything was piled into the back of Steptoe's lorry. Lovely.

Next time the developer visited the place, though, he hit the roof – all the stuff Steptoe had away is worth a small fortune and Dave was told, "You don't give nothing away for nothing. Get it back."

That weekend he was out drinking when he clocked Steptoe's son but it was not good news. The lad told him the gear was all gone and that was when the mist came down. Dave lost the plot and gave the poor lad one fucker of a beating. The wanker even bit off part of his ear. As the lad lay there covered in blood, the cheeky wanker finished off by stealing his Rolex Air-King (I've got a thing about watches and nicking that was bang out of order).

Steptoe came to see me when his lad was out of hospital and asked for a bit of help. His son will recover and a bit of plastic and glue will fix his ear, but it's the watch he wanted back. It's personal, and something that's been in the family. Can I help? Ten grand if the Rolex is recovered.

It seemed a piss-easy job 'cos it wouldn't take me long to ask around and find out where this Dave hangs out. It would be easy to persuade him to behave.

Sure enough, a couple of days later I was parked outside his gaff with me pal Sam for a bit of moral support, if you know what I mean. We had the address but it was one of those three-storey blocks with six flats in so we had to wait and see if we could spot him coming out of the right one.

Now Sam's a cracking lad, very handy, but he does like a joint. So we were sitting there in my little Astra (still making my way in those days) and he lit his first one up. The clock ticked on but there's no sign of Dave. Sam lit another. Tick tock. Then a third. Fucking hell, I had to get out of the car or I would have been as stoned as him and talking just as much bollocks.

Then a taxi rolled up and it looked like him.

"Come on Sam, game on lad," I said.

Sam rolled out of the car and before I knew it he stood in the middle of the fucking road, arm out like bloody Hitler, shouting "Stop, police!"

The driver wound down his window and took one look at the state of this obviously stoned idiot.

"You're having a laugh mate. This Jeremy Beadle or what?" he said.

By this time I could see the passenger ain't our man. Fuck.

So back to the Astra and Sam lit up again. Shall we call it a day or give it one last try? Bollocks we'll knock some doors, I decided. I dragged Sam out of the car and off we went to the block of flats, and climbed the stairs to the top level. Taking each in turn we peered through the letterbox hoping we could catch our man. We were going to be lucky if we did, but we did know he had a girlfriend so that could help. On the ground floor, I peered through the letterbox when I clocked her. There was a long corridor and she went off to the right.

"Come on Sam, follow me," I said. "You go right, I'll check the other side."

In went the door and we charged in. I hope Sam understood, but it was hard to tell because he was so stoned.

I stormed up the corridor and ran into the living room and there was Dave. All 6ft 4in of him. And his three mates. They were all fucking giants. Shit, but don't panic, I thought, Sam had my back.

"Like biting kids ears off, do ya, ya prick?" I said. "Now I'll ask nicely – he'd like his watch back."

Too late, BANG. One of his mates took a swing at me, missed and I clocked him, straight on his back. Another dived in, same thing but this couldn't last 'cos there was no fucking sign of Sam. I thought I might have to do this by myself. Now it was full on with Dave and his other mate piled in. We crashed all over the place smashing stuff. Telly, windows, it's all out. Somehow I got them down just as Sam finally turned up and put them out.

"I'll have that watch thank you," I said as I took it off the prick's wrist. Sam and I walked out the flat, but, shit, half the fucking street is lined up outside. Quick, think.

"Those robbing bastards did me nan's flat," I said. "They took all her jewellery, everything. They had it coming."

Now it turned out there was quite a problem with break-ins in the area and it appeared I'd pointed everyone to who'd been responsible. So Sam and I staggered back to the car and buggered off as the mob charged into Dave's flat to carry on where I'd left off. Result.

Saw Steptoe the next day and handed him the watch and he passed over the cash.

Not sure Dave was left with any teeth. He certainly won't be biting anyone's ear, that's for sure.

CHAPTER 5
THE GEESE

Paddy came to see me. Usual story in his game, tarmac, but the numbers were big. He was hired by a big corporation to do the car parks in an out-of-town shopping centre (fucking hate the places). Anyway, he'd landed a £300,000 contract and surprise, surprise, they were trying to bounce him for £107,000. It's a fact these big companies with their fancy offices and shite piped music are the fucking worst. Just robbers.

Job sounded a good 'un – £5,000 upfront for expenses and 35 per cent of the money recovered. That'll please the missus, I thought.

Armed with the names and numbers of the directors, I drove down to pay them a visit. Outside there was lots of nice cars, Jags and the like, lined up, so clearly they were not struggling for a few bob. So I walked into reception and there was this lovely girl sitting there staring into space.

"Morning, can I speak to John Parker please?" I said.

"Can you tell me who you are please and what it's about," she replied.

"Shaun Smith and it's a personal matter. I just need five minutes."

A couple of minutes later I was led to meet the lanky prick in a black suit. He shook my hand but it was as limp as an old man's dick.

"How can I help you Mr Smith?" he said.

So I went through the routine – he owed Paddy, I took on the debt so he needed to pay me. He played it cool and said the story I was told wasn't right. He explained that he didn't have the time to deal with it then, so asked me if I could come back the next day.

No problem. So 24 hours later I returned, but this time I brought me pal Paulie with me 'cos I felt he wasn't playing me straight. Sure enough, the alarm bells rang as I pulled into their car park. The day before it was crammed full but now there was only one Merc and a blacked-out Range Rover. Sort of cars you use in my business.

As I walked into reception, it seemed the pretty little thing from yesterday had got the day off. Now sat behind reception was this bruiser of a fella. The only reception he's ever manned is standing outside a nightclub in a dark coat on a Saturday night.

"I think we're going to be having a bevvy," I said to the lad with me, which, where I'm from, doesn't mean tea and biscuits. You could fucking smell what was coming. I told him who we were but he already knew and just grunted for us to follow him through to Parker's office.

This time he had someone with him – a dead ringer for Buster fucking Bloodvessel. You know that fat git who fronted the shit '80s band Bad Manners? So this is how Parker liked to do business, is it? First, he took the piss out of Paddy and now he thought he could put the willies up me. Fucking cheek!

Parker kicked it off by going through the motions that Paddy's work hadn't been up to scratch, that car park bays weren't marked out properly, that work overran. I only half listened 'cos I was fuming inside at his disrespect and had half me eye on Buster Ballbag sitting there smirking at me.

"I think we'll be having that bevvy in a moment," I whispered to Paulie.

"Yup mate, looking forward to it," he replied.

Parker was blabbering on when I heard the door open and someone else walked in. I didn't turn my head 'cos I knew it was another pair of hands for Buster and his mate.

Buster's phone was now ringing as well, but he wasn't

answering and it really wound me up. Answer the bloody thing you prick.

After Parker finished, Buster couldn't help but jump in.

"So let me tell you what we are prepared to offer – jack shit. You are getting fuck all. If you don't like it, I'm the offer."

And his phone STILL rang.

Parker was clearly getting a bit nervous that it was all about to kick off – it was a bit late for that 'cos he brought the meat.

"Okay, we'll pay £25,000," he said.

"Will you fuck," said Buster, thinking he had it all under control. "This is what's going to happen and I hope you listen. You're leaving and getting fuck all." Still the phone rang.

I turned to Parker.

"This is not cool mate," I said. "You brought in some heavies when we could have just sorted this – and this guy is fucking really heavy. Now I ain't going anywhere without the full amount."

Buster thought this was his chance, got out of his chair and lunged for me. I saw that coming 20 minutes ago! Before he got anywhere near me, he was on the floor. One punch.

"Now answer the fucking phone," I screamed.

The two lads Buster had with him hadn't moved an inch. They saw him go down quicker than a tart's drawers. No thank you. Buster finally answered his mobile and is blabbering away when he suddenly stopped and handed it to me.

"Someone wants to talk to you," he said.

Fucking weird but hey ho.

It was only one of me best mates, who Buster works for. He explained to him that he'd seriously fucked up and so had Mr Parker. Parker was ready now to pay the full amount but he took the piss so the game changed.

"Two cheques, one for £150k, and one for £50k, which is for me," I said.

Paddy would be happy with that 'cos without me he'd have got fuck all.

Oh and the next day Parker had a gang of lads at my house at the crack of dawn laying a new drive for me and the neighbour. Only charged him £500. Looks great.

Now I have to confess it doesn't always go as easy as it did that day. Some jobs can bite you in the arse – literally.

There was this time a lad, Steve, walked in, who was out of pocket by seven grand. He tiled a roof for a bloke called Billy, but, after he finished, was told by Billy that his job wasn't good enough. He said he had to "black tar" the roof, which basically means covering it all over in pitch so you can't see if it was fucked up in the first place. Easy for Billy and saves him a bundle. He probably did this with every job he gave out.

"I've been to his house, knocked on the door but he just opened the window and told me to fuck off," said Steve. "He's just a big fat arrogant bastard. I reckon if you turn up, Shaun, he'll pay you."

Steve was clearly happy with my reputation, so I hoped this prick Billy was, too.

Steve gave me his number and I rung him there and then.

"That Billy?" I said. "You don't know me but you know my good mate Steve from Royal's Roofing. Now listen to me pal…"

At this point, Billy butted in and gave me all this bullshit about Steve having done a crap job. I don't give a fuck.

"Look, I need to see you," I told him.

"What do you need to see me for?" he replied. "It was a fucked-up job and he ain't getting no seven grand. Tell you what,

I'll give him £500 and that's it."

"So I'll come and see you and you can give it to me."

"Fuck, no need for that. I'll pay him by BACS. Why are you so eager to see me?"

And then the phone went down.

Two days later, Steve got paid £500. Time to collect the rest. I headed to his house and knocked on his door, but there was no sign of him for days. Then I got word of where he went. Now I didn't know what he looked like, only that he was a big fat fucker called Billy, so that's what I looked for when I got to this private house where he was doing a job.

There was a lad out the front who told me Billy was out the back. Can you go get him? I asked.

"There's someone here for ya called Shaun Smith," the lad shouted.

"Tell him I'm busy," said Billy.

Fuck this I thought, so I opened the front door and walked straight through the house into the back garden. There he was smoking and eating a sandwich at the same time. Sloppiest bastard you have ever seen.

"About this money," I said.

"I've told you I ain't paying ya," Billy replied. "Now fuck off, I'm calling the police."

Which is what the cheeky twat did. Fuck him, I went round the front and waited for the bizzies. Young WPC turned up and first saw him and then came to me. I explained the job as politely as I could, and the only thing to apologise for was going through the house. Billy made all sorts of shite up that I threatened to kill him, but what he didn't know was I taped our conversation.

"He's just a bullshitter and he's going to pay up," I told her. "It won't be today, but soon."

Billy saw me drive off so he thought it was all over. A couple of days later he even had the fucking cheek to text me.

"I hope you took that good advice of the nice lady copper to stay away from me 'cos you will get an injunction and you will get locked up," it read. "Looks like the ball is in my court, Big Chief, bye, Big Billy."

You fucking fat twat. I was fuming, proper fuming.

Somehow, someone robbed all his ladders when he woke up the following morning. Can't be a roofer without ladders. The bizzies gave me a visit but there's nothing to pin it on me. Billy thought their visit would finally put me down so he rang me.

"Ha ha dickhead, now you're fucked aren't ya?" he boasted. "I said you would get fuck all and if you come near me again the police will have ya. I win again Big Chief. How does that feel?"

Sunday night I headed back to his house late in the evening with me pal Gordie. I knocked the door and saw Billy stretching out of the upstairs window.

"Billy, it's Shaun," I said. "We need to sort this. Come on, let's talk."

"Oh hello Big Chief. Okay, go round the back and I'll let you in."

So me and Gordie walked through the garden and up to the back door. There was a noise inside like a "slap, slap" on a lino door. What the fuck's that? I expected Billy to come out for a chat but when the door swung open two fucking enormous white geese dived straight at me. It was like the fucking film The Birds! They were trying to eat me!

I've never been so fucking scared in my life. They snapped

and hissed and flapped. And they fucking hurt! Gordie came into the garden and they set on him, too. He was down and they pecked his face and head. They are vicious, vicious bastards. I was proper shitting it but at the same time it was so fucking ridiculous Gordie and I pissed ourselves laughing. We managed to get to the gate and stumbled into the lane but one of the geese was after blood and carried on chasing us until we legged it. You would have thought we were being chased by the Mafia or the Taliban.

We got back to the car and drove off and after a few minutes pulled over.

"Billy, the cheeky bastard, he's had us off there," I said. "He's played it well."

Then I got my first look at Gordie.

"Fucking hell mate, have you seen your face? It's like there are love bites everywhere, your neck, ears, everywhere!"

As for me – there were so many holes in my trousers it looked like I'd been shot with a thousand pellets.

"Whatever you do, Gordie, don't ever tell anyone we've been had off by two mad fucking geese 'cos we'll never live it down."

CHAPTER 6
THE £700,000 DEAL

I was in the office one day enjoying a nice cup of tea and a Kit Kat – just two fingers, never four – when the phone rang with the offer of a job in Oldham.

The client was a Pakistani lad, let's call him Mr Khan, who was given my name as someone who can sort out little problems.

To be honest, his call couldn't have come at a better time 'cos I'd "been away" for a few months, if you know what I mean, so money was a bit tight. In fact, I drove around in a poxy little Astra, which normally I wouldn't be seen dead in. Not my style at all.

Mr Khan didn't want to give me the full details of the job over the phone, just that someone he was in business with owed him a lot of money and refused to pay it back. You've come to the right place, I told him, so we agreed to meet the next day in the bar at the Midland Hotel right in the heart of Manchester.

Now I've had some very nice jobs in my time with great pay days, but when we met up the numbers Mr Khan laid out were way off the scale.

"Sean, very nice to be meeting you, I am hearing a lot about you and I am needing your help," he said. "I lent a friend £700,000 and for a while he was okay paying, but now isn't. He owes me £450,000 and I'm getting nowhere. Can you help me please?"

Ding fucking dong – 450 grand! The fucking Astra's going for a start. If he's got access to that sort of money, this job is going to be fantastic.

"No problem, Mr Khan, of course I can help, just leave it to me and we'll have your money back in no time," I said. "First I have to explain my terms, which are an initial £10,000 engagement fee to cover my expenses and 35 per cent of any money recovered. Are you comfortable with that?"

He could walk away now if he wanted and I could see he was

a little bit uncomfortable 'cos it doesn't take a genius to work out my percentage would be just over £150,000 in my pocket.

Thank God my terms didn't scare him away 'cos he wanted to play and we shook on it. Happy fucking days are here again. Time to get to work.

The debtor was a guy called Mr Kemal and over the next month or so I did some serious homework. Fuck this job up and the missus would kill me.

Kemal borrowed the money to invest in some building projects in Pakistan, and persuaded Mr Khan there would be huge returns on his investment. Now I don't know much, but just looking at the news on TV every day might give you a clue Pakistan isn't one of the safest places in the world to invest your money. For months Kemal told Mr Khan that everything was fine when in truth the projects hadn't even got off the ground and seemingly never would. Kemal realised this before he spent all of Mr Khan's money and, thankfully, looked for something else to invest in. Turns out he's now turning a good profit buying and selling aviation fuel, which Mr Khan knew nothing about. He did now, though, and that's great news for us 'cos with the money Kemal had coming in he would have the cash to pay us back.

With my homework done I set up a meeting with Kemal at his office in Oldham. I made up some story about having money to invest, just to make sure he would take the meeting. He was all happy faces when I walked into his office, thinking if he did this right he would have more money to play with.

His fucking chin hit the floor, though, a few seconds later when, not one to hang about, I got straight to the point – where's Mr Khan's fucking money? What the fuck's going on?

He was all over the place and blabbered on at a hundred miles an hour about having no money and about all these problems in Pakistan he was having that delayed the building projects. As if I care about his fucking life story.

"Fuck those," I told him. "You're in the fucking fuel business now and you're making a bundle with my man's money. Don't fucking try and deny it 'cos I've got all the paperwork to prove it. Game's over son."

He was virtually in tears at this point, shaking his hand and muttering away to himself.

"Now here's what we'll do, Gupta," I said. "I'll be back on Friday to give you a bit of time to get some cash together. Don't be disappointing me now 'cos I'll be very upset to come all this way and you have nothing for me."

I came back on Friday morning but the cheeky fucker was nowhere to be found. It was only the following week after door-stepping the place round the clock that he finally turned up.

Here's me in my little Astra and Kemal's behind the wheel of a brand new fucking Range Rover. No money, my arse! I'm clearly in the wrong fucking job here, I thought, as I quietly followed him into his office.

His arse fell out his trousers when he saw me.

"I'll have those fucking keys for starters, lad," I said. "Where the fuck have you been? You think I'd not be coming back, you twat?"

But as he blabbered away his mobile rang. What he didn't know is I had one of me lads knock his door at home – nice house, electric gates and all that bollocks. It was his wife ringing and she was in a bit of a state 'cos me mate – nice fella, about 6ft 4in black guy – was on her doorstep talking about debts and her husband, and she was scared shitless.

Kemal ended the call. The point had finally got through.

"I pay you Monday, no problem," he said.

"Last chance lad. You fucking try and pull another fast one and me and you are going to fall out."

This time he was as good as gold and Monday morning hands over 50 grand in cash. Do you know how long it takes to count that sitting in the back of a car – all 50s, 20s and tenners? Fucking ages. But fucking great too 'cos that's me first £17,500 in the bag.

And so it goes on for weeks. I'd turn up and Kemal handed over either five, 10 or 20 grand, whatever he was able to raise. I was not going to press it too hard 'cos the money was coming in and me and Mr Khan were happy for it to go on like this.

But then I turned up this one collection day and this time Kemal was nowhere to be seen again. At first, I'm not that concerned as up 'til now he had been a good boy. I let it slide for a week and thought I would pick it up next Monday. But when I called again it was the same thing and this went on for a month. I give Mr Khan a call to explain why he ain't been getting his cash.

"No problem Shaun, I'm sure everything will be fine. Please don't be worrying, it's okay," Khan said.

Something ain't right here – why was he being so fucking relaxed? By my reckoning, he was still around £180,000 in the hole. I had that horrible feeling someone was taking the piss.

I left it for a couple more weeks but it nagged me. Fuck it, I drove over to his house to see if there was anyone at home. Lovely house just like me mate described, but this time it's not Kemal's wife who answers the door, just some cleaner.

"Hello love, is Mr Kemal at home?" I said.

"Sorry love, he's gone away to Pakistan on business," she replied. "Went with his wife and another couple, the Khans. Do you know them?"

What the fuck? Was he in fucking Pakistan with my fucking client? What the shit is going on?

"Sorry love, do you know when he'll be back?"

"Yeah, sure, he gets home next Sunday. I'm just making sure everything is nice and tidy here."

Sure enough, I stick a couple of lads at Manchester airport on the day they're due back and there they came waltzing through arrivals. Happy fucking holidays, you pricks. Now that I know they're the best of buddies again I got a couple of my lads to tail them for a few days 'cos they're bound to meet up at some point when a surprise visit from me may be in order.

A few days later they turned up at a textile factory in Oldham which, as it turned out, is owned by Kemal. I got the call from my lads and hotfoot it over from Warrington with me mate Titch riding shotgun.

This time we didn't knock any doors, just barged straight into the factory and there was the two of them right in front of us. Fuck, when they took one look at me their faces looked like they'd been caught watching porno by their mum.

"Now what the fuck are you two fucking pricks playing at?" I shouted.

"Mr Shaun, Shaun, please, please don't be shouting, we can explain."

"Well someone fucking better had 'cos I ain't happy."

Together we made a bit of a noise 'cos all over the factory these heads started popping up, around a dozen old Pakistani fellas who must have thought someone was trying to rob the place 'cos they all headed our way screaming "Bloody bastards, bloody bastards."

Shit, this could get a bit out of hand. It was like that bit in the Khartoum movie where General Gordon's about to get fucked.

"Titch, outside, and calm those old fuckers down will ya while I talk to these two pricks," I said.

Now Titch is a very big lad and the grandads got a bit nervous as he stepped in front of them.

"Now let's be good old gentlemen and calm down. We're just having a chat upstairs. Let's settle down please."

Good lad to have around, Titch. He gave me time to get talking and Khan quickly spilt the story. Kemal had contacted him and promised he'd pay off the remaining £180k but would do it direct to him – no need to have me turning up and taking a cut every few weeks. Despite everything I'd done to get him his money back, Khan took the deal stupidly thinking I'd take it on the chin and walk away. Fuck off, I still had £63,000 on the table. If Khan wanted to save money he could do it somewhere else, not out of my wallet.

"Your choice pal," I told him. "You can collect your money yourself if that's what you want but there's no way I'm not getting my share. You wouldn't have had a fucking penny off him if it hadn't been for me. You hired me and you knew the price. I don't give a fuck which of yez pay me but no-one's taking the piss. I can stay in your life or you can pay me the money."

He looked at Titch outside and me sitting there ready to stay there all day if necessary. Khan's call.

"Okay Mr Shaun, we will pay."

I got me first Merc from that.

There was another Pakistani lad I did a job for, Mr Hussein, who, unlike Khan and Kemal, was one of the nicest fellas you could meet. Smashing lad, in his late sixties.

He'd leant a guy £3,600 on the promise he'd be paid back the following week. Instead of the cash, though, he thought he'd get away with paying in kind so sent Hussein a load of towels and tablecloths.

"I don't want merchandise, I want my money," said Mr Hussein. "You can keep half the cash and, to be honest, if he gives you a hard time you can keep the bloody lot, Shaun. I'm not hard up and desperate for it, but it's the principle. I want to send a message that me, Mr Hussein, is not here to get ripped off. I have been in business a long time. I'm not here to be conned by this cheeky bastard."

Next day I went down the M6 with me pal, Andy, to a small industrial estate in Walsall armed with the debtor's name – let's call him Shiraz – and I knew he drove a blue, four-door Mercedes AMG.

We blagged our way into his office saying we had come to pay a bill we owed, waving an envelope we stuffed with tissues. Nice one that, always gets you through the door waving an envelope that looks stuffed with money.

Shiraz was sat behind his desk when he opened the envelope and quickly realised there was a game on.

"Who are you, what do want?" he shouted. "Are you gangsters, hard-case villains? Do you bring trouble to me in my office? You sneak in?"

As he ranted away I spotted them – the keys to his Merc. I had to get them somehow 'cos if he didn't pay up, it would be payment in kind, just like the fucking sheets he tried to fob Mr Hussein off with.

I tried to explain we were there for Mr Hussein's money but like all of them he was in denial.

"I give you nothing, Mr Hussein is bloody liar, I owe him nothing," he said.

"Remember the last conversation you had with Mr Hussein," I told him. "When he got the Koran out and you swore on it and promised to pay him his money back, like we swear on the Bible?"

"No, no, no," he said, going all fucking chapati. "Your Bible nothing, trash. You want trouble, you want trouble, you get trouble. Abdul get the guns, get the guns."

And with that he grabbed the desk and tipped it arse over tit. Andy didn't move but I bent down – 'cos the keys to his Merc landed right by me feet. I'll have them thank you very much!

"You bastards, you get trouble," he said, ranting. "I know SAS!"

"That supposed to scare us mate? 'Cos we don't do the running, we do the chasing. Fucking SAS bollocks."

"Not bollocks, I know guy in SAS and he come here if I call him."

So he rang the fella and yeah, he's ex-army but he wasn't in the regiment. Andy then piped up. He remembered he had a mate down in Birmingham who used to go around bragging he was ex-SAS.

"Is his name Peter?" Andy asked Shiraz, and showed him a number on his mobile. It was the same one Shiraz rang. "He ain't going to help you because he's our mate."

At this point, Abdul came back in with a little black bag. We didn't know if there were guns in there or not but best not to push it, I thought. Shiraz knew we had blown his chance of calling in the cavalry so if there weren't guns in his bag he would have to make us an offer.

"£1,000 take it or leave it," he said.

"You give us £1,500 and we'll fuck off," I said.

"No, I am not making a deal."

"What do you think we're on? Who Wants To Be a Fucking Millionaire? Phone a friend, 50/50, ask the fucking audience? Tell you what, fuck this, we'll come back when you've got some sense."

Andy and I got up and walked out to the yard and there, right by the door, is Shiraz's Merc, waxed clean, beautiful. I was straight inside and locked the doors, started the engine and hit the revs. Shiraz spotted me through the window and came charging out screaming bloody murders 'cos his car was about to disappear.

"Get out, you steal car, get out. I get the police," Shiraz screamed.

"Get the fucking police you prick," I said. "You threatened us with guns you twat and I've got it taped on me phone. £1,800, think about it. Five more minutes and it's two grand."

To give him a moment to think, I turned the radio full blast but it was set to a bloody Pakistani station and the noise was something awful.

Shiraz weighed up his options but he had no choice. He went back to his office and returned with an envelope with £2,000 inside.

Of course I took the cash, but to be honest I would have much preferred the car.

CHAPTER 7
THE IRA

In this game, you never really know how a job will pan out. It could be a simple knock on the door and job done, or one that gives you nothing but grief.

Take the time this lad came to see me, Kevin, who'd got himself in a bit of bother. He was in business with two partners, construction, and for a while, things had been great with lots of work coming in. Then when the crash came and the whole world ground to a halt suddenly, they hit the buffers and had to call it a day.

One good thing in their favour was that when they shut the company, it had no debts and in fact, quite a bit of assets – £135,000 worth made up of three wagons that were on finance along with a digger and trailer.

Kevin's story was that he'd been reluctant to shut the business but his partners wanted to just cut and run. Thinking the good times would return, he decided to set up on his own and told his mates he would continue paying the finance on the gear they'd bought and then split the remaining assets with them – £40k to one partner and £30k to the other.

"I started the new company and, as luck would have it, I'm doing well," Kevin explained. "Now one of the partners has come back and said the work I've got I already had in the bag when we were winding down the old company. He's saying I've pulled a fast one, which is just bollocks. I'll admit the work I've landed was a possibility before, but my partners knew that. It's not my fault they didn't stick around. They wanted to just cash in and walk away."

So why were his former mates getting so wound up? How much work has he landed? As it turned out, we're not talking a kitchen extension here. Seems he landed a couple of big contracts worth one and two million each, including one for building a 26-house development. Serious money, and that's why the ex-partner was knocking his door.

"He wants half a million quid," said Kevin. "He's convinced those jobs were in the bag when we were all splitting up. But I said to them in a solicitor's letter that there were a few jobs coming our way and asked whether they wanted to hang on. But they were stubborn and wanted out. I've told him he's not getting it but now I've had these Scousers on the phone threatening me. I've already given them 20 grand."

What? Back up a minute. How do you get to handing over that amount from a phone call? Kevin was clearly way out of his depth and needed my help desperately.

He told me the story of how he took a call from some guys who said they were working for his partner and he stupidly agreed to meet them. On his own. Late at night. He got into a black Audi Q7, blacked-out windows, of course, thinking he would be able to explain exactly what had gone on and that would be the end of it!

"I got in and, as I sat in the back, the guy in the passenger seat pulled a fucking gun on me," Kevin explained. "He told me I owed his mate £500,000. Shaun, I'd never seen a gun before, only on the telly. I shit myself. I tried to explain that I had the documents to prove I didn't owe anyone but he just kept on. He goes, 'We don't want any bloody paperwork, we're not solicitors. We want the fucking money. End of. And if you're thinking of going to the police forget it because we'll just come to your house and burn it down with your kids in it'.

"Then they rang the next day demanding I started paying. They wanted 10 grand by Friday, so I gave them it. I thought it had all gone away as I didn't hear from them for about two months.

Next thing I was just leaving my local after a pint and outside there's the Q7 – beep, beep – and they called me over. I had a couple of pints, okay, so I wasn't thinking straight and stupidly got in. Straightaway one of them said, 'Where's the money?'

"It was probably 'cos of the beer but I told him to fuck off 'cos I hadn't heard from them for weeks and thought it had gone away. Even when the guy pulled out a gun again I said it wouldn't work this time, I wasn't paying them anything and then he just smashed the thing straight in me mouth.

"Stop wasting our time," he said. "Give us another 10 grand and we're gone." So I did.

"I hadn't heard anything from them for about three months until this other fella called Chaser called. He said, 'Listen you, you gobshite, you owe 500 grand. I'm coming to see you and you're going to pay me'. It was fucking scary."

As soon as he said the name Chaser I knew this was a game-changer. I know this lad and he's a serious player down South. Kevin was swimming in very deep waters. Chaser goes after everything, a tenner, a grand, it's all the same to him – he chases fucking everything and can be very dangerous.

Unbelievably, Kevin told me he fucking agreed to meet Chaser. He'd have been better emigrating.

"When I met him he pulled up in a Bentley Continental with the roof down and this 30-stone lad in the back," Kevin explained. "I got in the passenger seat and he drove for 45 minutes down the motorway before pulling off down some country lanes. Then he stopped. I honestly thought they were going to kill me. This guy Chaser and the big lump in the back dragged me out the car and Chaser started shouting, 'Listen you prick, you owe me 500 grand and I'm going to get it. How do you think I wear £700 shoes, drive round in a £90,000 car and wear a £30,000 watch? It's 'cos I get conning bastards like you to fucking pay me'.

"With that, the big fat fella smacked me round the head and I'm on the floor. Next thing I knew he got his dick out and pissed on me. He goes, 'If you fucking move I'll put this in your fucking mouth'.

"Then Chaser came back and said, 'This is how serious we are. You're going to pay us you fucking little twat 'cos if you don't your wife, your kids and your house are getting torched. Do you know who I represent? I represent the Real Fucking IRA. I'm going to put you on to one of them if you fuck me around'.

"Shit, Shaun, the fucking IRA. What the fuck? Then he passed me his phone and there's this Irish voice and he said, 'Listen, you be a good boy and pay these guys, understand? Now if you don't, I'll be sending a couple of me own lads over to see yer and they'll be bringing you back to me in a suitcase in fucking bits and pieces'."

Now my all-time favourite film is The Long Good Friday. Bob Hoskins, bloody brilliant. Always thought it was a shit ending 'cos it looked like the IRA had won. Could be interesting this job, I thought.

First question.

"Kevin, did you agree to pay the guy, Chaser?" I asked.

"Course I did," Kevin said. "I've got to start next week with 50 grand in cash and then the rest is all to go into an account in Ireland."

I explained to him the 50 grand would be Chaser's money for delivering the message and that the rest was going over to Ireland into the IRA's bank account. Before I agreed to get involved, I wanted to make sure his story was straight so I sent him home to bring back all his paperwork. No point putting myself on offer if his story was a load of bollocks. Sure enough, though, he fucking didn't owe anyone anything, he already paid 20 grand to this little Scouse firm and now that bully from London wanted another 50, let alone the fucking IRA! Chaser was on the phone to Kevin every day, too, threatening to kill him and his family if he didn't pay up.

Right, time to take control of this, I thought. First thing was to keep Kevin as far away from everyone as possible. From here on in, it would just be me doing the talking and the first conversation was going to be with Chaser.

In my world, everyone knows the key players so when I placed the call to Chaser he knew precisely who I was. When I told him I was representing Kevin he was not happy 'cos all of a sudden his job got a lot more difficult.

"Shaun, can I be dead straight with ya?" Chaser said. "There's serious people involved in this deal. Take my advice and keep your nose out of their business, Shaun, and they'll keep their noses out of yours."

"This is my business," I replied. "Kevin's a mate and I'm looking after him now."

"Nah, fuck off, Shaun, this is just another job to you."

"Listen, it's not a fucking job, I do genuinely know the lad. It ain't happening. Understand, it ain't happening."

"Shaun, listen. Take this as a friendly, friendly warning. These are the fucking IRA. Serious people. They'll send fucking someone to chop you up and..."

"Yeah, I know and put me in a suitcase and send me back to Ireland. Why take the chance sending me back? Why not just chop me up and throw me in the fucking Mersey?"

"Shaun, these people are the real deal."

"Real deal Chaser? I know you know real people but you know fucking bullshitters as well. Whoever you need to talk to just tell 'em this game is over."

I hang up and, only a few minutes later, my mobile rang and surprise, surprise, there's a very Irish voice on the other end. Very naughty of Chaser to have given these nutters my private number.

"Now then Shaun, how yer doing?" the guy on the phone said. "Listen very, very carefully."

"Go on, I'm listening," I said.

"I don't know who ye' ar and I don't care who ye' ar but what I do know is where ye' ar, what you've got and where you go and where ya put ya head down at night."

"You fucking threatening me? Just let me get a word in. Are you threatening me?"

"This is a warning Shaun."

"No one warns me. I don't take warnings."

"Listen when you pick the phone up and you use your fingers to dial a number, they'll go first."

"Yeah, go on. And when I use me hand to pick the phone up me arms will go, I stand up to answer the phone me legs, they'll go next. I already know the script mate. I know the talk, it doesn't fucking impress me."

"Well what will impress you? When your wife goes shopping this week, I'll have a couple of Irish lads bump into her."

"You know what mate don't fucking ring me, don't speak to me, you aren't getting jack shit. You can go and suck me fucking cock."

"God forgive you, Shaun, you're a very silly man and your kids are going to be without their dad and your wife is going to be a fucking widow. This is what is going to happen."

And the phone went down.

Fucking Chaser, he gave them my number, the prick, so I called him back.

"Listen you, you fucking big gobshite," I said. "You gave my number to the fucking IRA. What you fucking playing at?"

"I told you they were serious people," Chaser said.

"I'm telling you what I told them, go and suck me fucking dick."

"I fucking will when they chop it off."

"Fuck off ya divvie."

All night my mobile rung, and I realised I had to be on me game for this job. I changed my routine, left home and arrived at the office at different times – all the stuff you'd expect. Some poor Paddy came to my gym one day and I was convinced he was their man. He was seconds from an intensive discussion when a lad I knew walked in and started chatting away with him. False alarm, just an innocent punter.

After a couple of weeks, it all got a bit boring so I decided to put a lid on it. I rang Chaser and set up a meeting. I needed to get his Irish friends' attention that if they were thinking of sending a squad over, I could handle them. Maybe they thought I was just a gobby Scouser with nothing to back it up.

Chaser and I met at a park in Leeds. He was nervous at first, and not sure how I was playing it. After a few minutes, I gave him the idea I was now ready to play and deliver the money.

"Can you get your IRA mate on the phone now," I said. "I just want to say something to him."

Chaser made the call.

"Hi boss, I'm with Shaun now, he wants to make a payment," Chaser said.

"Oh I didn't say anything about making a payment," I said to

Chaser as he held the phone. "I just want to sort it."

Chaser didn't have a fucking clue what was going on.

"Tell him I'll ring him back on your phone in five minutes with what the deal is," I continued.

As soon as Chaser ended the call, BANG, I clocked him straight on the chin and down he went. He's got a big rep, Chaser, but remember he needed his big fat twat to sort out Kevin. He wasn't man enough to get up.

He was groaning when I grabbed the phone from his pocket and pressed redial.

"Chaser, Chaser, is that you?" the guy on the other end said.

"No Chaser can't fucking speak at the moment because I've just knocked the fat twat out," I said.

"Yer what?"

"Chaser is lying on the fucking floor with his tongue in the air."

"Listen Shaun, you're now a dead man. I am coming for you."

"Listen to me, you're getting old, mate. This isn't like the old days 'cos the IRA I know would have tapped me on the shoulder and said, 'Next time we pay a visit either have our money or you'll go in a bag'. That's the way you should have done it you gang of fucking amateurs."

"I will find out everything about yer Shaun."

"Do it. You want to come to my town with yer fucking Irish accents, strange cars hanging round me house, fucking good luck. You've no chance you twat so fuck off."

Chaser was waking up so, fuck it, I hit him again. Time to go home.

Now as you can see I'd convinced myself the guy I was dealing with wasn't the fucking IRA, just a lad from down south.

Just in case, though, I took the name of the guy I spoke to on the phone and Googled it when I got back to the office.

Ouch! He's fucking fully paid up with the boys in balaclavas and is just out of jail on a licence. He just did a stretch for something about garden shears and a particularly painful operation with someone who'd upset him. Fuck, how was this going to end?

There's the luck of the Irish and this time it appeared to have rubbed off on me. Two days later me phone went and the Irish voice was back.

He made his calls and discovered we shared a close mutual friend – Joey, seriously busy lad – who'd been going through some desperate family shit where I'd been helping out. He vouched for me and gave me a clean bill of health and asked them to back off.

"Hello Shaun, I told you I'd be doing me homework and good for you I did as it turns out you're not the idiot I took yer for," said the Irish voice. "And Chaser, turns out he's not the man we thought he was over on your little island. In fact, we prefer the way you do business, Shaun. How about being our boy over there?"

Challenging offer!

"Thanks but not at the moment ta. But you can always ring and it may be there's a job I can help you with."

"You take care, Shaun, we'll be in touch. And say hello to yer mate Kevin for us. Tell him he can sleep easy for now."

Thank fuck for that!

When I broke the news to Kevin, he was over the fucking moon, so much so he dropped 50 grand on me as a thank you. Have to say I bloody deserved it!

CHAPTER 8
THE JUNKIES

Every now and again I surprise myself. I set out with a goal, am convinced I'm not going to be sidetracked, but then something happens and it's a new script.

There was a pub I ran years ago, lovely place and I was quite happy pulling pints and having the crack with the regulars. Nothing special, but good days. Then one night some prick broke in. It was easy in those days 'cos the windows weren't like they are now. All you needed was a screwdriver or a chisel and you could prise the glass out of the frame. Dead easy, so I'm told.

Whoever robbed me did the one-armed bandit in the bar and took the money out of the pool machine. Didn't touch the booze, which told me straight off it was a probably just a smackhead looking for a few quid so he could buy his next fix. Cheeky fucker 'cos everyone knew me in the area and no-one in their right mind would have come within a mile of the place if they weren't desperate.

I wasn't that arsed about the break-in, but the following week he was back again and this time overstepped the mark. On the bar, I had one of those charity collection boxes for The Little Sisters of Mercy. As it happened there were these three nuns I knew from a convent called Sister Lucy, Sister Vincent and Sister Stanislaw. Not normally the type of people I kicked around with but, for nuns, they were okay. The three sisters would come to the pub every other week to collect the money and always took the time to chat and have a laugh. A million miles away from the pub talk you get day after day.

I remember one time Sister Vincent saw I had a new BMW parked outside the pub and next minute she asked for the keys and was off down the road like shit off a shovel. Now some fucking smackhead had nicked their money and I'm not happy.

I put the word out that I want the thieving bastard's name. It only took a couple of days before one of the regulars walked into the pub with the guy's name and address. Time to pay him a visit, I thought, and like the nuns, he'd better have said his prayers.

I made sure the pub was looked after and jumped into the car with me mate Joey. Better to be on the safe side 'cos the address I was given is on a shitty estate. Some of these smackheads – and the people who deal to them – can be fucking dangerous. If they're off their faces, they can be a right fucking handful.

Half an hour in the car and we got to the address. The guy we were after was in a flat on the fifth floor of a tower block. Just as you'd imagine, the lift didn't work, there were no lights in the hallway, the place stank of piss and there was graffiti everywhere. Home sweet fucking home.

Joey and I made our way up the five floors and, after catching our breath, Joey said he thought he could blag his way inside by pretending to be another smackhead looking for a fix.

He rattled the door and shouted through the letterbox, "Let us in man, c'mon man, I need it, I'm hungry, I'm hungry, let us in."

Joey must have spent some time round these people 'cos he's got the way they talk to each other nailed. Joey banged away for five minutes but there was nothing from inside so we decided, fuck it, and kicked the door down.

It was pitch black inside and I could hear me feet squelching on the floor. What the fuck was that? The place stank – it was like the inside of a fucking public lavvie that hadn't been cleaned in years.

Joey was in front when he put his hand on a door handle, opened it and suddenly we were in the living room. A bare bulb that hung from the ceiling lit up the lad we were after. He was squatting on the couch dressed just in his pants, knees up around his ears and filthy. He was like one of those people you see coming out of a fucking concentration camp.

"Here lad, what you after?" he said.

He was so off his fucking head he still had a needle hanging out of his arm and it was fucking filthy. His skin was yellow and there were scabs all over him.

With the light on I could see now why the carpet's sticky – 'cos it was covered in, like, an oil. It was the stuff that spills off the spoon when druggies light the heroin. I'm heaving.

If this wasn't bad enough, there was suddenly a noise to my left and this creature came out from under the sink, you know like Smeagol in Lord of the Rings. She was naked, tits down to her belly and her skin was yella, too. She had the bushiest fucking moggie I've ever seen in my life. It's like she had Bagpuss stuck between her legs.

"Ee are lad, it's Shaun innit," she said.

Fucking hell, I knew her. She was part of a family I knew who came to the pub. She staggered across the room and sat next to her fella. She was as out of it as him. She rambled and begged me to leave her lad alone.

"I just suck cock for rock, Shaun," she said.

She opened her mouth and it was like a mouthful of Sugar Puffs. But you know what? That's when the plot changed – I knew this girl when she had her shit together. She came from a really nice family who always played it straight. How the fuck did she end up here?

This was rock fucking bottom. Look at them, look at the place. How fucking desperate was this? I left them with Joey for a minute to have a quick look around 'cos God forbid there was a kiddie in there. No fucking way could I leave it. There were no lights anywhere else so I used the torch off me phone to look around. In the bedroom, there was a mattress on the floor covered with shit and piss stains, blood and needles. No kid, thank God and nothing else, either. No furniture, no clothes anywhere. They must have sold everything for smack. They've got absolutely fucking nothing.

The Little Sisters would have been proud of me 'cos you know what I did next? I went in me pocket and took out £100.

"Listen, do me a favour, take this and get yerself sorted," I said. "At least get some fucking clothes, will ya."

Now I knew they'd just go and buy some more smack, but at least they wouldn't be robbing someone for a couple of days.

CHAPTER 9
THE INSURANCE SCAM

Get your bird a good kitchen and you're fucking laughing. A very good mate of mine, Dave, bought this old house cheap, and it didn't need a lot of work on it except for the back kitchen. He worked away a lot of the time so to keep his missus sweet, he decided to splash out on a top kitchen: granite worktops, marble floor, top of the range Aga, the lot.

He called in this firm to do the work and, with a bill for 30 grand to complete the gig, the one thing he expected was a five-star job. Not a chance. When they came to sign it off, there were cracked tiles on the floor, a leak from one of the pipes and scratches on the work surfaces. To make matters worse, when the job finished Dave was overseas working and it was down to his wife to try and get things sorted. She had the builders out a couple of times but the simple fact was the money was in their bank and they basically couldn't be arsed.

She rang Dave to tell him she was getting nowhere when he came up with the solution.

"Ring Shaun," he told her, "and get him to sort it."

Now there's nothing I hate more, as you know, than an arrogant piss-taker. The guy who ran this little kitchen company was exactly that.

When I rang him up, I told him that I was Dave's brother and that I was dealing with it 'cos he was away working. I could tell from the minute he started talking he didn't give a fuck. It's only when I said there was an inch of water all over the kitchen floor that he agreed to send a couple of lads out.

I dashed round to the house 'cos I knew if it was just me mate's wife dealing with it, they would probably fix the leak and fuck off.

"Hey up, is the kettle on?" said this fucking cheeky little

fucker as he walked in with his apprentice. What's there to be so fucking cheerful about? The kitchen was drowning in water.

"Forget the fucking kettle, mate, just fucking get on and fix this fucking leak, will ya," I said, fuming.

They saw I wasn't amused so they fucked off with their tools and after 20 minutes fiddling away at the back of the washing machine, the leak was sorted.

"Now, what about these cracked floor tiles, lads? What you doing about them?" I said as they were finishing up.

"Sorry mate, can't help you there," the older one said. "We're just plumbers. We can't be fucking around with marble, fucking expensive this stuff you know."

"I fucking know that. Me brother's spent 30 grand on this lot and look at the state you've left it. It needs sorting, fucking quick."

"Look, we'll take a few pictures to show the boss what you're on about and he'll call you, okay?"

"He better fucking had."

Sure enough an hour later the prick was on the phone.

"Eh, is that Shaun? Here's where we're up to mate," he said. "The leak we won't charge for but to replace all the tiles, I'll tell you in a nutshell – to rip them up, cement new ones back in and polish them up you're looking at another £1,500."

Piss-taker. £1,500 for replacing tiles they'd cracked themselves!

"Listen mate, I'm not a fucking idiot," I replied. "You've been out eight times now to fix things your guys fucked up. Are you fucking joking?"

Now this is one fucking arrogant bastard I'm dealing with.

"This is what I'm going to do and you can take it whichever way you want. It's £1,500 and with that I'm letting you off the VAT. That's all it's going to cost and that's all I'm prepared to discuss on the matter. You have a lovely day and ring us when you're ready."

And then he put the fucking phone down on. The cheeky bastard. Is he having a laugh?

An hour later, I pulled up outside his shop with one of me mates, Dickie, who rode along for moral support. The prick knew my name but not what I looked like so I went in and asked for the boss.

"Jonathan?" said this young spotty kid in a suit.

"Yeah, that's him," I said. "Can you tell him Shaun would like a word?"

The lad walked to this big glass office at the end of the showroom and there was the boss sat with a couple of customers. The young lad was back in a flash and said the boss was busy and wouldn't be free for at least an hour. Could I come back tomorrow?

Fuck that. So with Dickie in tow, I walked straight into the office to get his full attention.

"Excuse me, Shaun is it?" he said. "Didn't you get my message? Can't you see I'm busy at the moment? Could you please leave?"

"I'm fucking busy, too, mate," I replied.

Then the woman sat there piped up about "how rude" I was, barging in.

"Rude? Fucking hell girl, if you knew what this bunch of robbing bastards are really like you wouldn't be signing any cheques for this lot."

Now this had finally got the boss's attention 'cos he knew if I went any further with what a fuck up they'd made on Dave's kitchen then these new customers would walk straight out the door. So he called one of his assistants over to take the customers out so he could deal with me on his own. As he walked them out of the office, I saw my chance: I spotted a set of car keys – for a Jaguar – on his desk and, while he walked past me, slipped them into my pocket. An old trick I had done before but always worth trying if the opportunity presents itself.

On the way in I spotted this gorgeous red Jag Mark II. It'll be worth a fortune now, I thought, and someone's pride and joy. It turned out to be Jonathan's but when he walked back in he launched straight into me.

"How dare you come in here and try and ruin my business?" he said. "Who do you think you are?"

"Fuck you, you prick," I shouted. "You'll have no fucking business left if you don't sort me out. You've done a shit job on me brother's house and you're going to fucking fix it. I want someone down there this afternoon fixing the fucking floor – and there'll be no bloody bill, understand? If you want to fuck me about, fucking try it, I might have a surprise for you. End of."

"Surprise! Get out of my office or I'm calling the police now."

"Mate, you'll be getting your surprise in about one minute when I walk out this shop. Come on Dickie, this fucker's not listening."

We marched through the shop and into the car park as the prick glared through his office window. That's when I pulled the keys from my pocket and waved them in his face.

"Nice car mate, but my car now you prick," I shouted and then legged it across the car park and jumped into the Jag.

Beautiful it was, lovely leather seats, immaculate inside. Just the job except for a child's seat in the back.

I put the keys in the ignition and I was off as the prick and one of his lads came racing out the showroom and, bringing up the rear, was this huge woman who was a fucking Hattie Jacques lookalike. The three of them chased after me shouting "stop, stop" but I'm off, foot to the floor. Time to show them how I do business. They ripped off me mate with a 30 grand kitchen and now he wanted more to put right the work they fucked up.

I drove to a mate's car lot about an hour away. He's not too fussed about paperwork when it comes to stuff like this and I knew he could move a Jag like this pretty quickly if we had to. Time to ring the prick.

"Right this is dead easy," I explained. "Five grand and carry out the job you fucked up and you can have the fucking Jag back. Don't pay and it'll go missing. You'll never see it again. I'm going to text you an address where you can collect keys but you only get them for the cash. Simple. If you want to ring the police, ring 'em, 'cos I ain't arsed."

Bit risky putting myself on offer to the bizzies, but I bet he loves his car more than getting the pleasure of seeing me get my collar felt. Sure enough an hour later two of his lads turned up at the car lot with an envelope stuffed with the cash.

As I'm counting it out, one of the lads piped up.

"You took his car, didn't ya?" he said. "Fucking great, we hate the twat. Can't get a tea break on jobs, he's always ringing moaning and there's no overtime. He's a fucking miserable twat. I'm made up you've stuck one to him. He loves that car more than his kids."

The kitchen was fixed the next day and when Dave came back a few weeks later, we split the cash.

I love jobs that go easy like this but cars haven't always brought me luck. Me mate Bob bought this Frontera jeep on finance – big deposit then £200 a month 'til it's paid off. Times got hard and suddenly he struggled to make ends meet so he offloaded the jeep to another lad for a grand upfront plus the remaining monthly HP payments. There was only about two grand left to pay.

The loan company knew nowt about all this so a couple of months later they wrote to Bob 'cos the monthly payments weren't going through.

The trouble started when he called the lad he sold it to.

"If you don't make the payments I'm taking it back," Bob said.

"You ain't taking fucking nothing mate," the lad said. "I've given you a grand and I made four payments and that's all you're getting."

Brave words 'cos Bob can pretty well handle himself. If that's how the lad wants to play, sod it he decided and made his point clear by planting one on his nose.

"Miss one more payment and I'm taking it fucking back. Understood?" he said.

Now sometimes Bob can get ahead of himself and be a real smartass. More often than not it backfires.

After his words on the doorstep with the Frontera lad, he decided to pull another fast one. He kept a spare key for the Frontera and a couple of nights later crept round to the lad's house and had it away. And guess what? He found another buyer and sold it again – same as before, a grand upfront and the new owner carries on the HP payments.

All's going well 'til the first buyer is sat in a mate's car and spots his nicked fucking Frontera at a set of lights!

"Hey you, you cheeky twat!" he shouted to these two lads in the Frontera. "That's my fucking car, what are yous playing at?"

"Fuck off it's ours mate," the bloke said. "It's not fucking stolen."

"Look, here's the key, it's my fucking car."

They'd all got out and within a few minutes, Bob's brilliant scam had been laid bare. All three of them went straight round to his flat, barged in and gave him a seriously good kicking in front of his girlfriend.

Now you'd have thought Bob would've learned his lesson, especially as both buyers told him they'd be coming back 'cos they wanted their £1,000 deposits back. Not a chance in hell, even if they hadn't given him a kicking. Bob's put his thinking cap on and remembered he was still the registered owner of the Frontera and down as the borrower with the finance company. What did he do? He still had a spare key to the car and this time he broke in, poured petrol into the air vents and sent the whole thing up in flames. Insurance payout to the registered owner – five grand. Happy days.

Of course, it didn't take a genius to work out who'd sent the car up in flames and the next day Bob had both lads back on his doorstep demanding their money. That's when he rung me, his own 7th Cavalry, to come straight round and help him out. They were still banging on his door when I pulled up.

"Go on, fucking say it now you pricks, say it now, here's our Shaun," he shouted at the lads as I stepped out of my car and headed up the path.

One of the lads turned round.

"Who the fuck are you four eyes, sticking your fucking nose in?" he said. "Called you in for back-up has he?"

Before I could say a fucking word, the other lad swung a punch out of nowhere and clocked me bang on the side of me head, right on the frame of me glasses. You cheeky fucking bastard. The red mist was 'ere and I went from Dr Jekyll to Mr Hyde.

The one who hit me thought I was going to go for him first but fuck that, I thought, I'll take his mate out 'cos he's not expecting it. Bang, one punch, fucking poleaxed him.

"Come on, come on," said the other one but he was backing away all the time the little shite. Different story now ain't it when you're on your own?

"Fuck off, come here you little prick," I shouted. "Fucking steal a punch off me will ya?"

But every step I took forward he took 10 back and then he was off on his toes as I chased him like a fucking screaming lunatic. It took me three fucking blocks to get him, but I was so out of breath he only got a few digs.

"Now listen, this is what we're going to do," I told him. "I don't give a fuck what's gone on with the car or who owes what. You're going to get back in your car with your mate and you'll fucking stay away from Bob. Do you hear me?"

As it happened his mate had already done a runner. When he woke up from the haymaker I'd landed on him he said to Bob, "Who's that fucking lunatic with the gigs on," and ran for his car.

Bob was made up as you'd expect 'cos all his problems were sorted, but all I wanted to do was get back to my pub and calm down.

It was only a few days later on the Sunday afternoon when I was sat in my garden that it dawned on me. Bob had two fucking grand in deposits off those lads. He had an insurance cheque for five grand coming, and, okay he had one good kicking, but he did well out of it. Me? I've had someone steal a punch of me, had it with two fuckers and run through the streets like a fucking idiot. And Bob was sat there waiting for his money. Who's the dickhead here? Me. He drank in me fucking pub, I just battered two fellas for him and all he said was thanks. Bob, cheeky twat.

But I'll bide my time, I thought, no need to rush things. Bob now reckoned he was me new best mate so I played along for a couple of months.

"When you get your insurance cheque Bob I want to see it before you cash it 'cos I can't believe you're going to get away with this mate," I told him.

Sure enough, pool night at the pub came along and Bob was bragging he had the cheque in his pocket and the silly prick waved it around. Whoosh, it was in my pocket.

"Listen you cheeky twat," I told him. "I've made enemies over you being a prick and you think you're walking away with all that money and me getting nothing! Not over my fucking dead body mate. Here's what we're going to do. I'm holding on to the cheque and in the morning we're going to cash it together. All right?"

Next morning we're at this place in North John Street in Liverpool where we cashed the five grand cheque. Robbing bastards charged us £300 just for the fucking privilege. I reckoned with the two grand he'd already nicked off his two buyers, Bob could make do with another £800. Hardly 50/50 but he wasn't going to argue.

Funnily enough, he didn't come in me pub after that.

CHAPTER 10
THE DOGGING SITE

You know those nights when you can't sleep? Tossing and turning with a million things going through your head? I can't stand it so whenever this happens to me I'm up and about. I can get me zeds another time.

This is how I came to be on the road in the early hours one morning, heading down to Nottingham and the lovely Colwick Hall hotel. I'd booked six rooms there for a Saturday night for the team and me because we were running an event in the city. With luck, if I got there at about 3am then maybe a room would be free and I could catch a few hours before the others arrived later in the morning. They're not going to charge me extra when I've got six rooms on me booking, are they?

Now Colwick Hall is famous for being the ancestral home of Lord Byron, who's apparently a famous English poet who Google tells me was big in the Romantic movement. Good luck to the lad. Anyway seems romance still attaches itself to his old stamping ground, particularly the woods nearby the hotel.

I bombed down the motorway and only stopped at a garage for a coffee, paper and Kit Kat (two fingers straight away with the others in the glovie for the morning). Next thing I made my way to the hotel down this dark, wooded lane. I'm not going too fast 'cos a deer or something could jump out in this sort of place. It wasn't a deer that leapt into view, though – it was this bloke and a woman, and she was riding him like a jockey at Aintree!

What do ya do? Slow down, speed up or beep the horn? He kept to the same pace and, as I drove by, fucking gave me the big thumbs up! Next minute, what the fuck is that? There's another fella. This time he had a bird laid out on the bonnet of his car.

This time I threw the full beam on to show 'em I could see them and perhaps they'd like to move. Not a chance. The fella waved his arm up and down, all the while still going at it with his bird. He wasn't waving me off – he was waving me down to stop. Doggers! What the hell? This is not right, this. This can't be fucking right. The guy was now off the girl and stood in the road, forcing me to pull up. I wound down the window.

"Hey mate, you having a go?" he asked.

"Na, no thanks mate you're alright," I replied.

I had me latte with extra milk, me paper, me Kit Kat. That's all I wanted. Fuck that shit. Before I could pull away, there was another four coming up the road – two guys and two girls.

"Hiya," said one of the girls through the window.

"Hi," I said.

"Oooh, is that a Scouse accent I've just heard? I love Scouse fellas. Would you like to come for a walk with us?"

"Am I fuck love. Ta-ra."

Window up, and off I went a short distance to the hotel. Lovely night porter there, smashing fella.

"What the fuck mate?" I said to him. "What's going on round here? Fucking bodies everywhere!"

"Oh that's nothing sir," he said, laughing. "It's a famous dogging area near here. You're early still. Wait till the clubs kick out about 4am, then it gets busy."

Apparently, if you're in your car with the light on inside you're signalling anyone can come inside and join in. Light off all you do is watch. Fucking weird some people.

Anyway, I asked the lad if there was any chance of a room but the hotel was rammo and the best he could offer me was a couch in the lounge. I fucking hate sleeping on couches – it does me back in every time.

Fuck it. I'll sleep in the car, I thought. So I got back in the

Rover and drove to the far end of the car park. I thought I would just have a read of the paper, drink me coffee and eat me two fingers of Kit Kat then try and get a few zeds. Happy days.

I was there no more than 10 fucking minutes and what happened? A fucking white Ford Cougar parked up, this couple got out and the guy tapped on my window. What the fuck did he want?

He must have been at least 6ft 6in. God knows how he managed to fit into the Cougar. He was one of the weirdest looking people I have ever seen, like someone stretched him out on one of those medieval torture racks. I was pissed off at this point because I just wanted to eat my Kit Kat.

"Hello, I'm Simon," said the guy, who I'd now named Stretch Armstrong in my head. "Me and my friend want to know if you would like to have some fun? There's plenty of room in the back of your car."

He said all this with a stupid fucking grin on his face.

I wanted to pull his arm into the car then drive off with him hanging out the side, but thought better of it. It was too early for that shit and I do like this hotel, so I decided to pull away and leave them to it.

Anyway, you may be wondering why a debt collector is talking to you about driving past a dogging site in the middle of the night? Well here is where it gets interesting.

A friend of mine called me up a couple of weeks later and said some guy in Nottingham had knocked him for a few grand on a property deal. I wouldn't normally entertain such small amounts, but he is a pal and if I can help out those around me, I always will. I met him at a pub in the centre of town and he went through the details of how this estate agent was supposed to pay him a commission on a house that got sent his way.

The deal went through fine but the slippery fuck estate agent decided he didn't want to pay the £4,000 commission he promised. So he got his phone out and showed me this guy's Facebook page.

The second I saw the picture I had one of those moments where I thought I saw him on the telly or that he might have been at my school. And then it clicked – it was Stretch fucking Armstrong from the hotel car park! I cracked up laughing and my mate asked me what was up.

"Two weeks ago that guy came up to me with some bird and wanted to dog," I said.

"What you mean, Shaun?" he replied.

"Dogging, you numpty."

"I didn't know you were into that Shaun."

I stopped laughing and gave him a dirty look. I explained what had happened the other night in the car park and it was a complete coincidence that I had bumped into this Simon.

As we flicked through the rest of his Facebook, it became evident that Stretch lived a double life. Happy at home with the kids and wife and not a hint that he was going for a midnight drive for a spot of dogging.

This was more a bit of fun for me now, but I told my mate to get a pal and pop down there over the weekend again. Wouldn't be too hard to spot a giant in a white Cougar rogering some middle-aged woman.

It took them a couple of weeks but they managed to get some photos of him with someone doing the dirty. That's the thing about sexual deviants – once they get a taste of something they like, they will keep going back there till they find something more entertaining.

We got the photos printed, then I called up and asked for Simon and picked out a house I wanted to view. I went with another friend to view this six-bed house in the country about 30 minutes from his sex patch.

You could tell from the start he was a bit nervous – maybe he recognised me from the hotel? Probably not. It was most likely having two intimidating looking guys in a house with him in the middle of the country.

"What is the local area like?" I asked him.

"It's lovely and peaceful, great local amenities, a real country vibe but still with great links to the city centre," he replied in his estate agent bullshit.

"That's great, but what about anything a bit livelier?" I asked, smirking. "You know for when the missus goes to bed."

"Oh well, there's some great pubs around here and again the links into…"

I cut him off.

"What about dogging spots?"

His face dropped faster than his passenger side window would on a Saturday night. We got the pictures out and explained that he shouldn't make promises he didn't intend on keeping.

A week later my mate was paid and I had a cracking story to tell the boys back at the gym.

CHAPTER 11
THE BENT BIZZIES

In my game, it's only a matter of time before the work I'm doing is going to bring me into contact with the bizzies. Trust me, over the years we've had a lot to talk about and on the odd occasion, they may even have been right to start the conversation. But honest, I ain't lying when I tell ya I've dealt with so many bent coppers I could start me own force with them.

I did a bit of filming a little while back for a production company who wanted to do a fly-on-the-wall documentary on how I go about my business. Usual stuff, nothing too tasty but seemed to go down well on the old YouTube. That led to another firm coming along and asking if they could do the same thing again, this time for Channel 4. Few quid in it for me so no problem: lights, camera, action, as they say. As it happens, having a film crew on hand was to come in very handy.

The night I was down in Nottingham dodging the doggers, four of the boys in blue turned up at my home to serve a "notice" on me. Four of 'em – to deliver a piece of fucking paper! My girl, Amanda, wasn't going to tell them where I was 'cos she knew I was working and didn't want me troubled by the bizzies suddenly turning up. All she told them was they could catch up with me first thing Monday morning at my gym. I'm usually there before 6am ready to teach a class for some of the lads. As soon as the bizzies fucked off, Amanda was straight on the phone and filled me in on their visit. Okay, so they want to serve some bit of paper on me, then why don't I get the Channel 4 film crew along and they can record the whole thing? Should make for some interesting telly 'cos I can guarantee the coppers ain't going to like a camera pointing in their direction.

Monday morning, Ed the cameraman was there in plenty of time and wired me up with a microphone so he could record whatever was being said. It was not long before the same four bizzies rolled up and all four of 'em walked into the gym. I could see one of them wore a small body camera to record what was going on. Well, my camera was fucking bigger than his so we'll see if he liked that!

I was round the back of the club in the office when the bizzies walked in at the front and were immediately met by Amanda with Ed standing there with his camera. This wasn't in their script at all and they were clearly not happy when Amanda explained that Ed worked for Channel 4 doing a documentary on me and was filming everything that went on at the club. They were not sure how to play this so one of 'em got on the phone and called his boss, an inspector, back at the station asking how they should play it. They could carry on, he told them, on the condition Ed agreed that, if the footage was used, their faces were pixelated. Ed's not fussed either way so gave them a thumbs up, which is the signal for me to come and say hello.

"All right lads?" I said.

Straight off, no pleasantries, one of 'em piped up, "Can you just identify yourself?"

"Identify myself?" I replied. "I don't know who I am from one day to the fucking next mate. Who do I want to be today – do I want to be a nice guy or do I want to be a bad guy?"

To be honest I was already annoyed there were four of 'em there to serve a bit of paper on me but now seeing them standing there all cocky with everyone in the gym looking on, I'm not fucking happy at all.

"I woke up this morning a nice guy but you lot are probably going to make me a bad guy 'cos someone's told you a load of shit about me," I went on.

They looked a bit nervous especially with Ed getting right in close, filming everything. One of them moved forward and handed me the bit of paper. It's what they call a disruption notice. I knew what it was about now. There's a job I was working on in Liverpool where the guy I was chasing was playing it cute, giving me the runaround and telling me he had important friends who could deal with me and that I shouldn't be messing with him. Seems those friends are his mates in the police and he called in a favour to get them to warn me off.

One of the coppers blabbed on about how they could use this section or that section of the law to prosecute me if the "threats" didn't stop. In addition, they'd look at getting an ASBO to keep me away from the guy's home and work. They're complete dicks 'cos this is all a fucking sham and my lawyer would rip right through it. What about innocent until proven fucking guilty? How about listening to my side of the story?

Then they really overstepped the mark.

"If the threats continue we will notify social services that you are engaging in criminal activity and placing your children in danger," he went on. "We will also seek to evict you from your home and your work premises in case you bring the risk of violence there."

He then handed me the fucking notice and asked me to sign it.

"How does fuck off sound?" I said.

"Don't be swearing," said another of the bizzies.

"Wait there," I said and pulled me phone out to ring me brief. Ed's happily filming away.

The brief's advice was straight to the point – if they followed a procedure, there must be an official complaint on record. It's a bluff, he told me, there's no official complaint. Get them to arrest you 'cos they won't, they can't risk taking you back to the station 'cos this ain't official police business.

"After speaking to my solicitor and taking his advice, I don't have to sign jack shit," I told them. "And what I would like to do, officers, is ask why it takes four of yous to come here and see me. Scared I'd kick off were ya?"

I could see one of them was holding some paperwork, which had some of my experiences with the bizzies written down and the advice to "approach with caution" stood out at the top of one of the pages. I'll tell you about all that another time.

"I'm signing fuck all, so what are yous four going to do?" I said. " 'Cos you know what I'm thinking? I just hope to God yous want to try and arrest me. Do it, go on, fucking do it. Nick me. I want to be arrested. I want to be locked up because you and I know it's a load of bullshit. You fucking come in here, threatened to take me away from my kids, kick me out of my home and take me out of my business. Are yous for real? Just fuck off, I ain't signing nothing.

"You, you, you and you please leave," I added, as I pointed to them all individually. "Just fucking leave, get out of my face now 'cos if you don't fucking leave I won't be accountable for my actions. Get it?"

Ed's happily filming away and the four bizzies just looked at each other and knew they were fucked. Doing a favour for their mate hadn't worked out as planned and I've got it all on film. Fuck it, time to go home and they just fucked off leaving me with the unsigned notice. Wankers.

Back in the office, I had a cup of tea and a Kit Kat and took a proper look at the notice they handed me. Something was not right. Before all the legal bollocks, there was a line that said:

"To be headed on the force's paper". One of these fucking clowns had gone and copied the wording for whatever notice this was and just pasted it onto a bit of blank paper. He couldn't even be arsed to do a proper fucking job copying it on to fucking official force stationery.

I called a lad I know who worked with the bizzies and ran him through what happened and he asked me to scan the notice over to him.

He phoned me right back.

"Shaun, here's what's gone on," he said. "The lad you're chasing, he's obviously pulled in a favour from someone he knows in the force 'cos there's no way that notice should ever have been issued. We only use them for people like terrorists. We'd have people on 'em 24 hours a day, tapping phones, staking out their homes, everything. It would have to be signed off by the top brass and this has only got an inspector's signature on it. It's just bollocks. Forget it mate."

Normally I would have, but I was not ready to drop it. I had got the inspector's name so I would have a little chat with him, I thought. For three days I rang his office but he dodged the calls until I finally got through to him.

"Morning, Shaun Smith here," I said.

"What can I do for you, Shaun?" he replied.

He knew exactly why I was ringing, the prick.

"I tell you what you can do for me. A couple of things actually. One, why didn't your lads arrest me?"

"Shaun, we've got no need to arrest you."

"Hold on a minute, it's an arrestable offence to threaten someone isn't it?"

"It's an allegation, Shaun."

"Yeah, it's an allegation without foundation. Why did you serve me with that notice? You should have arrested me, banged me up for a couple of hours and given me a smack on the arse. Why didn't you do that?"

"Shaun, this is for your benefit."

"Oh is it? Threatening to take me away from me kids, from me business. Let me ask you about this notice you want me to sign – why wasn't it signed off by your chief superintendent and why isn't it on official police paper as it should have been?"

"Uh, uh, who told you that?"

"Half the fucking bent coppers I used to see take money on the sly. Yous are all fucking bent."

"Now hey Shaun those are strong words."

"Not words, facts. Now listen, you and I both know what's gone on here. You thought you could just send some of your boys round and wave a bit of paper at me and scare me off? It ain't happening. Do you want me to ring your fucking super and ask him why he didn't sign off this notice? He won't have a fucking clue about it and if it was genuine he should have."

This fucking prick knew he was in a hard place now. He had four of his boys on film trying to serve me with a notice you only get signed off if you're chasing one of those ISIS nutters. Little old me? Never.

If I make a complaint, his days in the force are over along with his four mates and he knew it.

"Er, Shaun, there seems to have been some crossed wires here, there's been a mistake somewhere."

"Too fucking right there's been a mistake. But tell you what I'll do – there's no need for us all to fall out over this. I'll make sure if we use the footage your lads' faces aren't shown and we'll keep everyone's names out. If your bosses see it and start asking questions they'll have a hard time tracking you and your mates down."

"That's great Shaun, very understanding of you."

"Listen, I'm doing you a big favour here and you fucking know it. I'll keep the bit of paper, okay."

End of conversation.

Not my usual style to help out the bizzies but you never know, may need a favour off these pricks myself one day.

CHAPTER 12
THE RING

I should have said no right at the very start – I could smell trouble straight from the off.

Sarah was a good-looking girl who came to my pub with her mates for the karaoke on a Sunday night. Not a bad voice but she'd never be another Adele, take my word. One night she came in early, saw me at the bar and asked if she could have a quick word. No problem, so I took her to the back room and straight away she was in tears, blubbing away that her mum had just died.

I know Sarah and her family – loads of 'em, got to be at least 10 kids and they all live in one of the dodgiest parts of town. It's real bandit country. They didn't have a pot to piss in, been on benefits most of their lives, ducking and diving when they got the chance.

Her mum dying was sad news but what did she want with me?

She quickly told me the story. When she died, the mum had only one thing of any real value – a diamond ring that had to be worth a least a couple of grand.

The alarm bells rang louder every minute as she carried on with her story. I knew straight away I shouldn't get involved 'cos family rows are a fucking nightmare.

What exactly happened then? Sarah was away when her mum took the last bus upstairs and for whatever reason wasn't around when her dad passed around the family bits and pieces his missus had left.

One of the brothers, Peter, had been handed the diamond ring even though he knew from the off his mum had wanted it passed down to Sarah. Knowing there'd be hell to play when she found out, Peter had done the gentlemanly thing and flogged the ring as fast he could. Fuck memories of his mother, the three grand he got for it was far more precious.

This job had shit written all over it 'cos what Sarah wanted, of course, was for me to knock on her brother's door and somehow get him to recover the ring and hand it over. Going to take my best powers of persuasion to get this hard-up Scouser to hand back three grand just 'cos he upset his fucking sister. But Sarah's a nice girl so I decided to give it a go, see if I could talk some sense into him.

Next night I got his address and drove out on my own to do the business. Ding dong. I rang the front door and he answered, trackies on, filthy vest, fat fucker just like his wife who I could see sat on the sofa, her arm elbow deep in a family pack of crisps. He was pleasant enough to begin with as I wormed me way into the house, saying I was a friend of his sister, sorry to hear about his ma and other bollocks. The fucking air turned ice cold though as soon as I mentioned the ring and that I was there to bring it back. His missus even stopped munching her crisps.

"Too late mate, I sold it to Maggie Kelly for £500 down and a hundred a week till she pays off the full three grand," he said. "You've got no fucking chance getting it off her."

Maggie fucking Kelly. Fucking hell, she's as mad as a badger on crack and so are all her family. That's not a door I really wanted to knock. This job was getting worse by the fucking minute.

His gobby wife started mouthing off as well. She must think she's got a bigger pair than her husband.

"Anyway what the fuck has this all got to do with you, eh?" he went on. "You some fucking hard man? Think you can come in 'ere and threaten us? Fuck off."

I could have kicked off 'cos I ain't threatened anyone, just knocked the fucking door and been polite, trying to do a girl a favour. Instead, I just left it 'cos I got what I needed and that was the buyer's name.

Saturday morning and I ain't knocking Maggie Kelly's door on me own, so I rang one of me mates to come with me, just for moral support you understand.

It was like fucking World War III out the front of the house. Bottles, bins, shit, shoes everywhere – fucking neighbours from hell and it was just as bad next door and every other house around. Fucking shithole. If she was living like this, where the fuck did Maggie get the money to buy the fucking ring?

Knocked the door and within a second there were a dozen voices shouting, "Get the door, get the fucking door." It's like that programme, The Waltons, where everyone's shouting from room to room – only swearing like fucking troopers. Eventually, the door opened and there's this little kid, can't be no more than seven, in his undies, hands in his pants playing with his little dick.

"All right mate, what is it?" he said.

"Is ya ma in?" I replied.

"Why?"

"Just tell me is your ma in?"

"Why?"

"I need to speak to her."

"Why?"

"Just get her will ya kid."

"Why?"

"Have you got a fucking parrot kid?"

"Yeah we've got a fucking parrot and a snake. We've got everything in 'ere you know."

Cheeky little fucker. But fair play he was holding door. Train 'em early round 'ere in case the bizzies or the like knock.

"Have you got an older brother lad? Go and get him if he's in."

"Yeah, I'll get our Stevie," and off he ran into the house.

I could see inside and up the stairs there were loads of kids heads peering down and someone shouted: "Don't let no-one in." Then all the bedroom windows at the front opened and there were more heads sticking out, waiting to see what's going on. Maggie had more kids than fucking Barnardo's.

Big brother Stevie now arrives in his trackie bottoms. I could see he was in pretty good shape, but not long out of school.

"Who the fuck are you mate?" he said. "Whaddya want?"

"I need to see your ma."

"Really, see me ma? Whaddya want to see her for?"

"It's between me and her. Is she in?"

"She's not fucking here, all right."

"When's she going to be back?"

"I don't fucking know. Could be today, tomorrow, five fucking years for all I know."

"Listen, do me a favour. Tell your fucking ma I want to see her and there's me number."

"Why?"

"Nothing to do with you."

And then out of nowhere the stupid fucking prick pulled a blade out of his trouser pocket and went for me. Fucking idiot. BANG! Down he went, three of his teeth, rotten as fuck, hitting the floor a second before he did.

"Tell your fucking ma to call me. Fucking pull a knife on me you arsehole."

With that, I fucked off and within an hour the phone went. It was Maggie.

"Is that fucking Shaun Smith?" she said. "You been in my house and hit my fucking Stevie?"

"Listen love he was coming on to me with a knife."

"No he fucking wasn't you fucking bully. You come back to my house right now. I want to know what this is fucking over."

"No problem love, on me way."

"You fucking better be 'cos I'm his ma and I ain't fucking happy."

Me mate's nervous 'cos he thought we were heading for an ambush but no worries, let's see how it plays out.

Back at the door, ding dong, and immediately an upstairs window opened and out popped Maggie's head.

"You Shaun Smith?" she screamed. "What do you fucking want?"

I could see Maggie's head, just about, 'cos her tits are fucking enormous.

"Am I talking to one of yous or three of yous?" I said.

"Fuck off. What's it about?"

"You bought a ring. It's got to come back."

"Fuck off has it."

"It has to love. Listen, you shouldn't have had it. The lad who sold it to ya was out of order. Now his dad is going to give you the money you've paid already, so calm down love."

"Don't fucking 'love' me. Who the fuck do you think you are coming round here and hitting my Stevie?"

"Listen, I'm not going 'til I get the fucking ring."

There were babies screaming in the back and she was getting wound up big time 'cos they wouldn't shut up.

"You want the ring do ya? Stay there. Just stay fucking there."

She vanishes from the window and a couple of seconds later she's back.

"You want the fucking ring, do ya? Well fucking 'ere."

And with that she threw this fucking shit-filled nappy straight at me. Fucking Phil Taylor would have been proud 'cos she hit me right on the side of the head and all down me arm. Fucker.

"You want the ring?" she shouted. "Well it's in the fucking nappy so fuck off," and she slammed the window.

I'm too worried about the shit all over me fucking head and arm to kick her door down.

"Get the fucking nappy, Macca," I shouted to me mate. "And give me your fucking shirt 'cos I fucking stink."

I fucking knew this job was shit right from the bloody start.

Couple of days later I was at Sarah's house with her dad to deliver the ring.

"Fucking hard job this one was – fucking load of shit chucked out of the window from that Maggie 'cos she wasn't happy," I explained.

They didn't have a clue what I was talking about 'til I pulled the shitty nappy out of a carrier bag.

"The ring's in there," I told them. "You can dig it out yerself 'cos I've had enough of dealing with this shit."

CHAPTER 13
THE CARS

Most people outside Liverpool have probably only heard of Toxteth 'cos of the riots in 1981. Seemed the whole country was kicking off at the time, people had had enough of Thatcher's Britain, especially the black communities that were getting a shitty deal.

In the years after the riots, the city spent millions trying to make things better, desperate to stop the violence from reigniting. You know it can only take one small spark and off we go again – fires in the street and bricks lobbed at the bizzies. Purely by accident, I was once very nearly that spark.

Our kid, Kevin, bought this lovely flat in Upper Parliament Street for himself and his girlfriend. This was a couple of years after the riots when the area was being smartened up but was still very much the centre of Liverpool's black community. I was living at home sharing a room with me nan so when Kev said he was going round Europe for six weeks, I jumped at the chance to babysit the flat. I already knew a load of the people in Toccie 'cos as a kid I had a job where I worked round there.

Anyway, I moved into Kev's flat with me girlfriend and it was like being on holiday. Time on our own and great for walking into town – for a young lad it couldn't get any better. The only date in the diary I had to keep each week was to make sure I got back to me ma's for Sunday lunch. Nothing wrong with that, especially as I could take a bit of washing back at the same time. I was really feeling like cock of the North at this time. I had money coming in, loads of work, a nice bird and an even nicer car – my bright red two-litre Ford Capri Ghia with sports wheels and blacked-out windows. It stood out like a whore in a convent when I parked up in Toccie.

I was staying in Kev's flat for a couple of weeks when one

of me mates, Tommy, asked if he could borrow the car. Tommy worked for me a couple of nights a week helping out on some of the doors I ran at a couple of the big clubs in the centre of Liverpool. I told him he could have it provided he delivered it back at our Kev's by 12 o'clock on Sunday 'cos I would need it to get back to me ma's for dinner.

Now just to let you know, I love a nice car but never get too attached to 'em. If I can move it on and make a few quid then happy days. So, I came out of Kev's flat on the Sunday morning when this Rasta-type walked up and started gabbing away about me Ghia.

"Hey mon, where's ya car, ya sold it mon?" he asked.

"Nah, me mate's got it, just lent it to him for a couple of days. He'll be back later with it," I told him.

"Great mon 'cos I's thinking of buying it if ya wanna sell it mon? C'mon how much mon?"

I only paid a grand remember, which was a lot of money in those days.

"£1,700 and you can have it," I told him.

"Ah, ya taking the piss mon? C'mon be serious. How about £1,500?"

In the mid-'80s a £500 profit was a fucking good deal so I bit his hand off.

"Don't you want to drive it first mate?" I asked him.

"Nah, I seen it outside yer flat mon and it's cool."

Now all we needed was Tommy to bring the car back. I was stood there with me new Rasta mate, Delbert, who it turned out lived in the same building as our Kev. Midday comes round but there was no sign of Tommy. Half an hour went by but he was still nowhere in sight and me fucking dinner was getting cold!

"Tell you what, Delbert, I'm going to get a cab back to me ma's," I said. "When I get hold of me mate, I'll tell him to drive round 'ere and drop the keys off. We can settle the money later." Sound.

I had a lovely bit of beef and a mountain of veggies before I got me head down for the afternoon. Before I did, though, I rang Tommy's home number but it just rang out. Fucking prick, last time he borrows a car off me, I thought.

The reason Tommy wasn't picking up the phone was that he was fast asleep at some bird's house in Bootle. When the clubs kicked out on Saturday night, he'd picked this girl up and been shagging her all night.

When he woke up, it was fucking nearly tea time and he knew he was going to be in the shit with me. He jumped in the shower, said goodbye to his bird and jumped straight into the car and raced round to our Kev's flat keeping his fingers crossed I'd not be too fucked off.

Now at this time of day in Toccie on a Sunday evening, all the brothers sit out on the doorsteps, smoke weed, chill and listen to reggae blasting out from the flats. Tommy pulled up outside Kev's flat and started banging on the horn thinking I was still indoors. Of course, I was still dead to the world back at ma's.

So what did the prick do? He jumped out the car, left the keys in the ignition, ran into Kev's building and up to the flat and banged on the door for a couple of minutes but got fuck all reply. The sound of him banging, though, got someone to the door of the flat opposite and guess who popped out? Fucking Delbert!

"Hey mon, you got the keys for the Capri? You can give me the keys mon," said Delbert.

Now Tommy's not the brightest lad and can sometimes make

too hasty a decision, but all he could see in front of him was this big Rasta man demanding the keys to the car. He thought he was being robbed. So he did what came naturally to many of us Scousers and landed a punch right on the side of Delbert's head. Sadly for Tommy, Delbert was still standing and he proceeded to kick the shit out of him as he chased him down three flights of stairs back out into the street.

That's when Tommy's day got even worse 'cos there's no sign of the car – some fucker had it away while he was upstairs banging my door. With Delbert not far behind, Tommy legged it down the road as the Rasta brothers cheered Delbert on like Romans at the fucking Colosseum.

Half an hour later, Tommy rolled up in a taxi at me ma's house and laid out the story. I could fucking kill him for being such a twat, leaving the keys in the ignition, what a divvie. But he already took a good hiding and another from me wasn't going to make much difference.

Right, time to think. Tommy said there were loads of Rastas sitting out in the street when he drove up – somebody must have seen who nicked the car. I ordered a cab but got another mate, Titch, to meet us at the flat.

Sure enough, when we got back to the address the street was still full of the brothers and sitting with them was Delbert. I thought maybe he had something to do with it, thought better of it and just had one of the brothers nick it so he could make a few bob.

As I walked towards them, Delbert clocked me and saw Tommie, who was last seen half an hour ago running for his life.

"Hey Shaun mon, what ya doing with dat prick? He ain't cool mon," Delbert said.

"Fuck cool mate. Where's me fucking car?" I shouted back.

"What ya on about mon? I ain't got no car."

"One of you fuckers had it away and I want it fucking back, okay?"

Delbert and his mates saw I was raging and they all got to their feet and it ain't in a friendly way. Hmm, I may have slightly miscalculated this, a bit like fucking Custer.

"Maybe you better take a walk mon," said Delbert, which is pretty good advice 'cos I could see Tommy already backing away, clearly not relishing a second kicking of the day and this time by a whole fucking mob of Rastas, not just one.

"Listen mate," I told him. "I'm going to have a look around and if the car doesn't turn up there'll be hell to play."

"Sure ting mon, you go have a look see and we be waiting for ya when ya get back. Be cool."

Me and the lads walked off down the road thinking we'd just be going through the motions 'cos the car's gotta be long gone. But then after just a couple of minutes, we headed down Granby Street and we suddenly spotted the Ghia parked up outside someone's house. Fucking cheeky twat this, nicks me car and just drives round the fucking block.

I went straight up to the door and gave it a knock with the lads sticking close behind me as another Rasta fella opened the door.

"Hey you, that's my fucking car!" I shouted. "You cheeky cunt, you fucking nicked it!"

"No mon, what ya talking about blood?" he replied, calmly.

"Don't take the piss mate – that's my fucking car, there, parked right outside your fucking door."

"You calling me a thief mon? 'Cos that ain't nice, you know."

He was squaring up now, moving out of the door. But behind him I spotted half a dozen Rastas suddenly appear out of the living room. Fucking hell, here we go, I thought.

I was all set for it to kick off when Tommy pulled me shirt and as I turned round there was about 16 Rastas getting into my fucking car.

"Oi, where the fuck do ya think you're going?" I shouted, but he was off like a shot with me and the lads charging down the road trying to catch him. We were so fucking raging we even picked up bricks to throw at the car as it raced away.

What the fuck? Me car's been nicked twice in one day. Fuck this, I thought, let's head back to Kev's flat and have a brew, 'cos it can't get any worse.

Delbert and his mates were still hanging around outside when we got to the flat and are about to go in when me fucking car suddenly came screaming down the road and pulled up right in front of us. Behind the wheel there was the cheeky little twat who just had it away down Granby Street.

I was straight to the driver's door and dragged the little gobshite out on to the pavement.

"Here you, you little twat, fucking nick me motor will ya," I shouted.

"Hey mon, what ya doing? That's me cousin mon, leave him alone!" shouted Delbert as his mates headed towards me. They clearly didn't like the idea of one of their brothers getting a smack.

"I don't care who the fuck he is mate, he's a little thief," I shouted.

"I ain't no fucking thief," said the kid. "Dis is me cousin's car. He's just bought it and I was taking it for a ride man. Honest."

Hold on a minute, I realised, come to think about it, he'd

have to be really fucking daft to nick the car and then bring it straight back to where he took it from. Let's give him a chance and let him explain.

"Mon, me uncle told me he bought the car and was getting the keys at lunchtime," he said. "When I sees it here 'bout six o'clock wid da keys in I's thinking da car is his so I's just taken it for a spin."

Fucking Tommy, this was all his fault for getting here fucking late. If he'd been here on time none of this would have happened. At least he already took a kicking. Thank God for a sense of humour 'cos I saw the funny side – we nearly started another fucking riot all because Tommy slept in.

"Okay man, let's forget about all this. You still want to buy the car?" I asked Delbert.

"Sure mon, come inside and I'll give ya the money."

Five minutes later the deal was done, he got the keys and the car was all his. We went outside so he could take it for a ride when he suddenly noticed something's not quite right.

"Woah man, look at da fucking car. What the hell happened mon?" he said.

Fuck, maybe it wasn't such a good idea to throw those bricks at the car! In all the commotion earlier we'd all missed the large dents in the boot and the crack running through the rear window.

"Blame your cousin man, not my problem," I said.

"Whadya mean blame him? Look at the car mon!" he shouted.

"Listen, if he hadn't been driving the fucking car we wouldn't have thrown bricks at it, would we? He shouldn't have fucking got in it, should he?"

"Are you crazy, throwing bricks at this beautiful car? Come on Shaun, ya gotta give me some money back, look at it!"

"Tell ya what I'll do. Tommy here will give you a couple of hundred quid. That should sort the paint job out. Can't do more than that."

"Hold on, why the fuck should I fucking pay – it's not my car," said Tommy.

"Listen, this is all down to you being fucking late, 'cos you copped off with some bird in the club and were wellying her all morning," I said. "You got a big snotty dick on yer and then yer turn up here late and me car's been fucking nicked and ya cause murder with a load of Rastas. 'Course yer going to pay him."

Me and cars, eh? Get me in no end of trouble.

CHAPTER 14
THE BRASS

I was sat at the bar one day minding my own business, reading the Echo, when in walked this lad I know, Frankie, and he came straight over to me with a little job he wanted taking care of.

Frankie's small-time, and makes all his money renting out shithole flats that only people who can't afford anything decent would ever take. He does a collection round every Saturday morning, calling on all his tenants, to take £100 cash off each. Nice little business 'cos the taxman is never going to know how much is going through his hands.

His problem was one of the girls who rented from him, Debbie, hadn't been paying and was now £1,100 in the hole. Now I know Frankie and this didn't quite feel right. At £100 a week that's 11 weeks he let this slide, which is a long time in his game. Normally he would only let it go for a few weeks and if they didn't make it up in arrears they were out the door. I could tell he let it slide for a reason, but at that stage, it wasn't my problem 'cos he offered me £500 to knock her door and get the money. If she refused to pay, I would throw her out. Simple.

I left it for a couple of days before I jumped in the car and popped round to knock her door at the time she'd be expecting Frankie to be doing his rounds.

Given the type of people Frankie usually rents to it was a bit of a surprise when Debbie opened the door. I expected the usual sort of scrote Frankie rented to – you know, shell suits and a can of lager in their hand all day.

But Debbie was a pleasant surprise – quite tidy, nice clothes, you know like a mate's mum who hasn't quite lost it all and would have been a real looker back in the day. I quickly explained I was a friend of Frankie and surprisingly she was pleasant and invited me in, which is odd for someone who's supposed to owe such a lot of money.

Again I was pleasantly surprised as the place was spotless, like a show home.

"Hey girl, do you really live here?" I asked. If she did she must be cleaning the place all the time, I thought.

"Yes, sure, but I work nights and just sleep during the day so the place doesn't really get used," she said.

"What are ya, barmaid?"

"Is that what Frankie told ya? Well, sort of, Jack of all trades really. Anyway, what's up? What can I do for ya? Got time for a cuppa?"

"Go on then girl, I'll have a cup, two sugars. You ain't got any Kit Kats have ya?"

She made the tea but there were no Kit Kats. Ah well, can live with that. Pleasantries over it was time to get down to business.

"Look, girl, Frankie's asked me to pop round 'cos you are going to have to sort his money out."

"What money? What you on about?"

"£1,100, it's got to be paid love."

"Sorry, what are you on about? I don't owe Frankie anything. If I did I would have paid him because I've got money, look..." and she then walked over to a cabinet and fetched a little vanity case. Inside there was about £700.

"Look love, if you've got the cash why haven't you paid? Frankie, he's been coming round every week hasn't he?"

"Yeah, for a fucking blow job and a shag! What does he say I owe him money for?"

"For your rent, 11 weeks."

"You're joking? Does he think he was getting a fuck for free every week? I've been paying him in kind and he knew it."

Frankie, you naughty, naughty boy, and very poor form not to have given me the full story.

"Look, Shaun," said Debbie, "I'll be dead honest with ya. I work in a massage parlour. I don't do the streets. I'm a high-class brass."

This has now turned into one of those few occasions when I felt distinctly uncomfortable. If she's okay opening her legs to pay the rent what she going to have in mind if she has to pay the debt Frankie insists she owes? She's a nice enough girl but, like I said, she looks like one of me mate's mums. She also couldn't stop talking and insisted on giving me the full story on Frankie.

"I was in bed one Saturday morning, bit of the flu, when he was at the door asking for the rent. Well, 'cos of the flu I'd been in bed all week and hadn't earned anything. So I told him I didn't have it but could I pay him double next week? Straight away he said there were other ways I could pay him. Seen one cock, seen 'em all in my game so I told him I could sort him out, blow him to kingdom come. Go on then, he says. So I did.

"Next week he was back again and this time I was the last one on his round. Now he asked for a cup of tea and a biscuit and a blow job and then the following week the full works.

"Last time he was here it was 11 o'clock and he came in shagging me, sleeping, shagging and sleeping and not leaving 'til 4 in the afternoon. To be honest it was a complete pain 'cos I was working that night and needed me sleep.

"Honest, Shaun, this is the truth. You think I'd be lying on me silly boy Frankie? And he's not going to like the fact I know what he's been up to on his Saturday afternoons. Certainly, his missus wouldn't like it and his mates would take the piss right out of him if they knew he was knocking off a brass. Down the pub he's making out he's a regular guy, loves his wife and kids, and all the time he's got this dirty little secret."

One thing I hate is when someone puts me on a job and doesn't give me the full story. Frankie should have come clean, so to speak, and as he didn't it was time to have a bit of fun with him. I decided to give him a call.

"Hello mate, no sign of this bird Debbie," I said. "I'll give it a while but it ain't happening yet. Hey, by the way, you know you said she was a barmaid? One of the other lads here reckons she's a brass. Did you know that 'cos she could be using the flat for her business?"

I could hear the panic in his voice. "Brass, nah, nah Shaun, defo a barmaid mate. Wait 'til you see her, you wouldn't pay a penny to shag that."

The best bit is that I had him on loudspeaker and Debbie was next to me! When she heard this, she was fucking raging and was about to kick off so I quickly hung up.

"The cheeky fucking bastard," she shouted. "He comes here every fucking week for a suck and a fuck. And he's shit at both – he comes quicker than the fucking AA. I'll fucking show him."

I was just having a laugh now but Debbie was seething.

"Not worth a penny," she said as she took off her top.

"Fucking bastard," she added as she pulled down her trousers.

"Come on Shaun, fuck me and tell me if I ain't worth it," she screamed as, finally, her bra and panties flew across the room.

She looked half decent with her kit on, but standing there starkers in the middle of the living room I could see why she works nights!

"Steady on girl, I'm just here for the money," I protested.

"Don't be such a fucking pussy, Shaun. Come on let's have some fun!"

"Sorry love, it ain't happening. Very kind of you to offer but no thanks. It ain't 'cos of what Frankie said but I've got me own bird and don't do this, honest."

"For fuck's sake, I can't even give it away."

"Don't take it bad, girl, if I was single no problem but I don't cheat on me missus. Look you go and get dressed and I'll fuck off and have a chat with Frankie, see if we can sort this out. Okay?"

"Whatever you want, Shaun. Fucking weird – every other bloke I meet wants to fucking shag me and all you wanna do is run out the room."

Having made my excuses, I returned to the pub 'cos there was still work to do as I hadn't earned a penny out of this. No way Debbie should be paying the full £1,100 given the amount of time she'd laid on her back for Frankie. In fact, I think it's him who should be shelling out for services rendered, but not necessarily to Debbie.

Couple of hours later I caught up with Frankie and pulled him into my office at the pub.

"Listen mate," I told him, "I know what's been going on and if it gets out, you're in the shitter mate. Debbie's told me everything."

"What, Shaun?" he said, sounding terrified. "What's she fucking said?"

"How you've been banging her for weeks. Everything, all your dressing up in women's clothes, high heels and stockings. You fucking weirdo. You're a fucking idiot, lad. She's a full-time brass and it's going to get out 'cos she fucking services half the bloody city and she's a mouth on her as big as the Mersey fucking tunnel.

"If I was you, I'd leave her alone, forget the fucking rent and move on. And you'd be wise to make sure she keeps quiet. I'd be giving her £500 to keep shtum, in fact I can guarantee she won't breathe a word if you give her that. Just in case, I'd be cutting the rent too, say £50 a week instead of a tonne. I can do you a favour and pick it up for you, which saves you having to see her again.

"Fucking hell, Shaun, could you? If my missus finds out I am fucking dead. It's bollocks about women's clothes, honest. She's just making that up."

"Doesn't matter lad. Once it gets out it's her word against yours and who's going to believe ya? You were fucking a brass mate, end of. Look Frankie, just give me the money and I promise she'll behave. Trust me."

"Okay, thanks Shaun, you're a real mate. I fucking owe you big time for this."

Happy days. Frankie's money in my pocket I headed back to Debbie's. Knock, knock, and she opened the door – thankfully fully dressed but the "come and get it" image won't get out of my head. Cup of tea and a biscuit, and it was time to wrap matters up.

"Right love, I've spoken to Frankie and he thinks it's best if you deal with me from now and we'll keep it strictly professional," I told her.

"Fine by me, Shaun, get me Saturdays back for a start," she said.

"Now you've got to admit love you do owe some money – you've got a lovely flat 'ere and even though you were letting him have a fuck, you've still got to pay something. You can't live here for free. Tell you what we'll do. You pay half what you owe to me today and we can call it quits. I've told Frankie he ain't going to get any more than that. He ain't going to be knocking your door again either 'cos from now on I'll be 'ere every week to pick up rent, which we'll keep at £100 – and no payment in kind, okay?"

"That's fucking great Shaun. You're a diamond."

No need to tell her about the rent reduction, was there?

You can't live for free, not all of it, but Frankie will settle for half. It's a good deal.

And the best bit is I'll be collecting the rent in future so there'll be no more problems – she can actually get a bit of rest!

Shaun the landlord. Good job.

CHAPTER 15
THE CLUB

You know that saying: "like herding cats"? Well, trust me that's a piece of piss compared with trying to look after a bunch of so-called celebrities living it large in a nightclub.

The clubs I used to look after could easily take in a couple of thousand kids a night and, except for the usual pissheads, punch-ups and pissed birds, they were pretty easy to manage. Most of the trouble normally happened at the close of play when the lads who hadn't picked up a bird ended up taking out their frustrations by battering the shit out of each other out in the streets.

This sort of stuff was run-of-the-mill and quite easy to cope with. The nights we all dreaded on security, though, were when we had guest appearances, such as some celeb coming to promote some song they had coming out or book they wanted signing. We all knew these celebs looked down their noses at the rest of us and, once they're fuelled up on booze or whatever drugs they've got stuffed in their handbags and pockets, well they can be a right fucking pain in the arse.

A classic example of this was when Katie Price, or Jordan as she was known then, descended on one of Liverpool's legendary clubs, 051, to promote some single she'd just released. I was running security at the club so the manager called me in to brief me on her visit, making sure I'd have everything in-hand to make sure she wasn't pestered by the punters.

The club promoted Jordan's visit for weeks so on the night she turned up it was absolutely rammo. She had a posse with her and from the minute they arrived you could tell they were in party mood. There was Dean Gaffney and Sid Owen, out of EastEnders; Kenny Dalglish's son Paul; and this porn star, Omar. (Imagine the length of a baby's arm, well that tells you all you need to know about Omar!)

Jordan's job for the night was pretty simple. She had a brief appearance on stage while they played her single then it was up to the VIP area, which overlooked the whole dance floor. Now and then all she had to do was wave to the punters below and, if she was up for it, get her tits out for the lads. Easy money – it's why the place was packed.

When she arrived, the manager introduced me to Jordan and her mates, explained who I was and that I'd walk her through the club and stay with her group all evening. As he was talking, all you could hear in the background was the DJ winding everything up, telling the crowd inside that Jordan had arrived and leading them in an Anfield-like chant, "Get your tits out, get your tits out, get your tits out for the boys, get your fucking tits out for the boys."

Jordan did not look amused and was even more unhappy when I explained we'd have to go right through the whole club, through all the punters, before we got to the stage. Lots of opportunity for some brave lad to try and grab her arse. As we went down the two flights of stairs into the main dancefloor, she looked petrified. Even with four of my lads up front trying to clear the way through the crowd, Jordan had her arms gripped around my waist and walked step by step with me, like in a three-legged race as we barged our way through. To be honest, I couldn't see what all the fuss was about 'cos once she got on stage all she said to the crowd was "Hi guys" and then sang a few lines from the song she was promoting. Trust me, Liverpool had heard a lot better. Stick to Page 3, love.

Job done, we were off the stage, charging through the crowd again and up into the VIP area where she could relax with her mates and drink unlimited champagne on the house for the rest of the evening. Given how many people had packed into the club to see her, the owners could easily afford to fill her up with plonk for the night. The VIP area could hold about 100 people, so the club invited some other guests up to join Jordan and her mates.

My job was to hang around to make sure everything stayed cool and everyone was looked after and that nobody got into any trouble. Having done this type of night countless times before, I knew it wouldn't be long before the champagne kicked in and someone started playing the arse.

Sure enough, it was only half an hour later when Dean Gaffney walked over to me and started chatting away as if I'm his new bessie mate.

"Hey Shaun, is it true what they say about Scouse birds, that they're easy shags?" he said.

Fucking EastEnders prick, always preferred Brookside meself.

"Is it true what they say about Cockneys?" I fired back. "That they're all little pricks like you?"

"Ah, come on Scouse, just having a laugh," he said.

I could tell he was bricking it a bit. Down South he probably never had anyone answer him back 'cos he's "a star". Well, not tonight son.

Couple of minutes later I see why Omar was at the party, as someone asked if he really did have a 12-inch cock. Omar's got his girlfriend with him but, given what he does for a living, he was not embarrassed and just flopped it out. Fuck me, you could roll pastry with the bloody thing. Thankfully, he quickly put it away before someone tripped over it, and carried on talking to his girlfriend, the lucky woman.

Jordan, meanwhile, tucked into the champagne and cuddled up with Dalglish Junior who looked like he was going to score easier with her than he ever did on the pitch. Not a patch on his dad who was a Liverpool legend.

All okay there, I thought, now what about the other two? Where's that prick Gaffney gone and the other lad, Sid?

I wandered down to the back of the VIP area where there's a dark section, like a chill-out area, but a lot quieter. Here they were. I could see the two of them crouched over a table, their backs to me and then the sound of a very loud sniff. Now, what could that be?

"Hey lads, you all right there?" I said. "Need a hand?"

They turned round like they'd been caught stealing from their mum's purse but relaxed when they saw it was me.

"Fucking hell Shaun, you fucking scared us there mate," said Gaffney.

"Now behave lads, you've got to be careful in here 'cos there's cameras all over the place. Why don't you just get back to the party, okay? And I'd wipe that shit off your shirts before you do."

Now they're not the first to do a line of coke in the 051 but there's a time and a place for this sort of thing and wide out in public ain't one of them. The two of them head back laughing to where Jordan's sat and were straight back on the bubbly, life and soul of the party again. Sadly it's not that long before I noticed the two of them had gone walkies – they're nowhere to be seen in the VIP area. What the fuck are they up to now?

A quick call on me radio to me mate John, who's monitoring the club's CCTV cameras, told me our likely lads were down one of the back exits of the club and this time they were with two of Liverpool's finest young ladies. For fuck's sake, if these girls were here with some local lads and they were now fucking around with these EastEnders lads, it would kick off.

With one of the other security team, I walked round to bring them back up to the VIP area. Shit, this time they were either side of the staircase, drinking away as the two girls looked as if they were about to perform a favour for their new-found friends.

"Hey, what the fuck are yer doing lads?" I said.

"Hey, Shaun ain't it? We're just having a laugh," shouted Owen.

"Fucking stop it will ya," I shouted. "I told yez there's cameras all over the place. You never know where this stuff could end up, in the papers?"

Ah, sense dawns. A Scouse nightclub in possession of footage of two young soap stars with two young girls about to get very close. Wouldn't look good on the CV when they're auditioning for the next part, would it? Time to behave, ladies, and for everyone to get back to the party.

"Come on lads, back upstairs, fun's over."

It's not that long, though, before I got a call over the radio that some people had gone out of the VIP area into a part of the building closed to the public. Off I trotted, up the stairs to where these guys are supposed to be and guess who – our two lads again with more lines of coke laid out than there are tracks into Lime Street Station.

"Whoa lads, what's happening?" I said.

Gaffney looked up.

"Fucking hell, you again," he said, looking startled. "Can't even get a line without you turning up. We don't get this shit in London. Why don't you just fuck off?"

"Don't get fucking lippy now, you cheeky little prick," I told him. "I'm not arsed about you picking up a bird if that's what she wants, or snorting. But I told you not in front of the cameras."

"Oh just fuck off. You're only a 10 bob, two-bit doorman."

That was it then and I grabbed Gaffney before he could even wipe his top lip.

"Here you, you cheeky twat," I shouted. "A fucking two-bit doorman? Just 'cos you've done a bit of telly work don't think you can come the big 'I am' with me."

His mate Sid backed away at a million miles an hour. If Gaffney wanted to get mouthy with me, that was down to him. Gaffney was still not behaving, though.

"Listen you, do you want me to get Jordan down? She'll sort you, we've earned this place good money tonight."

Sort me out!

"Right, empty your fucking pockets. Let's see what else Santa brought you for Christmas."

Three bags of beak and a couple of tablets – and they're not fucking paracetamol – appeared in his hand.

"Two-bit doorman, fuck you, you arrogant twat," and I grabbed the drugs, threw them on the floor and crushed them into the carpet. "Now fucking behave or fuck off."

Gaffney was clearly not used to not getting his own way 'cos he ran straight back into the VIP area and like a little rat whispered away in Jordan's ear and within minutes she asked for the manager.

"I want him sacked," said Jordan, pointing at me. "I want him sacked, out of this club now."

"Sorry, he's part of the club, it doesn't work like that," the manager said.

"Sack him or we're going."

"You can do what you like, love. Shaun ain't going anywhere. Your friends have been well out of order all night. If you want to fuck off, fine by me."

Nice when the boss stands by you and with that the party was over. Within a few minutes Jordan and her mates were packed up and gone – round the corner to another club, Garlands, where it just so happens I also looked after all the security lads. I was on the phone to them straight away to warn them what went on and to make sure they were on their toes.

Jordan was fucked off her party had been ruined, but once they were tucked into Garlands' VIP area, the party was soon back on.

Now one thing about Garlands is it's an incredibly old building, huge cellars downstairs, which is where the main toilets for the club are located. Also happened to be home to an army of rats that had overrun the place. If Jordan needed the loo, Garlands were going to have to make sure she was kept well away from the cellars.

After an hour or so hard partying, Jordan did ask where the toilets were, but it wasn't to go and take a piss.

At the 051 she and King Kenny's son had been turning each other on big time and at Garlands it had carried on full steam ahead. Jordan needed the loo but she took young Dalglish with her.

The only place the club had other than the cellars downstairs was a disabled toilet, which was right next to the club's massive main bar. Jordan got the key and in front of all the punters in the club dragged Dalglish inside with her. Interesting.

Now her performance back on stage at the 051 had the crowd going wild but this was nothing compared with the cheers ringing out in Garlands when the disabled toilet's doors swung open and there was Jordan and Dalglish wrapped around each other inside.

As the cheers rang out they suddenly realised the whole bar could see them and desperately tried to pull the door closed. Too late.

Tells you something about how thick skinned some of these celebrities are. When they emerged back into the bar it wasn't a case of hide your blushes, heads down and straight off home. No, back they went to the VIP area and the party kept going.

For me, just another typical night looking after "the stars". Give me pissed-up Scousers any time.

CHAPTER 16
THE SUBBY BASHING

Over the years the industry that has kept me the busiest is construction. Whether it's a little firm owed for building a house extension or a supplier who hasn't paid his bills, there's always money for me to run down and a few decent bob to be made.

Now and then a job drops into my lap that feels like a winning ticket on the lottery. The best are where one of the big boys, a national company, has done the dirty on a small contractor (the subby) who it hired to work on one of their major projects.

Couple of months ago one of these came my way when this client called and said he was chasing a million owed by one of the biggest building companies in the land. The firm is very involved in how the London skyline looks, and it's got landmark buildings all over the place. But I'll save its blushes and keep its name to myself (also keeps their lawyers off my back).

This job was quite typical of what goes on throughout the industry. The contractor – let's call him PLUM CONSTRUCTION – hired my client – we'll call him LEO LTD – to carry out a £12m build for him. This is way in excess of the sort of projects LEO normally gets involved in, which are usually £2–3m gigs.

Taking on such a huge job has put LEO out on a limb. There was extra staff to hire so the wage bill went through the roof, supply orders were massive compared with what it usually needed and the bank had to be friendly when it came to running their overdraft. So long as the money kept flowing from PLUM to LEO every time a bill needed to be paid then everything should be fine.

At the start of this project it all worked fine for LEO as whenever it shelled out for supplies, the company just invoiced PLUM and it put the same amount back into LEO's account.

It's only when the project neared completion that problems

arose, known throughout the industry as "subby bashing". PLUM knew exactly when the project was coming to an end and when the final payment – and profit – was due to be paid to LEO. Obviously, it would much rather keep the money in its own account so suddenly the regular payments LEO received hit problems; LEO was told the computer was down, someone wasn't around to sign payments off – you know the drill.

With its cash flow not running smoothly, LEO hit problems paying its suppliers so it started holding back on deliveries. Wages couldn't be met and lads left the job for other work. With the project running late, PLUM could now say there were problems with LEO not hitting deadlines so they started charging "penalties" for LEO being late. And on it goes until the bank got involved 'cos they can see where this is all going – tits up with LEO running out of cash and unable to cover its overdraft!

That's precisely what went on in this job and the guy who ran LEO knocked my door 'cos he reckoned PLUM turned him over and owed him a million. As ever, I was happy to oblige 'cos there's a lovely payday looming. He didn't pay my usual 35 per cent but with a promise of 50 grand if I could sort it, I was happy to take on the job. He also told me the names of six other firms who had all done work for PLUM and were in the same boat as him. Together they were owed millions.

LEO handed over all the paperwork on the job and within a few days I was on the phone to PLUM and managed to get through to the right guy. Now I was pretty sure he spent most of his time talking to public school City types in very expensive suits, so having a very plain-speaking Scouser has got his attention. He could tell straight away I've been around and knew exactly the sort of strokes his lot were pulling.

Better to talk face to face, I suggested, so the next week I was on the train down to London and PLUM's offices in Canary Wharf. Fuck me, its offices were more like a five-star hotel, the money it must have spent on the place – marble floors everywhere and weird fucking sculptures that probably cost a bomb.

I could tell when we sat down in his office he was ready to play ball. It was pretty obvious he did his homework on me. Probably just put my name in Google and found a bit of TV work I did that got millions of plays on YouTube. He wanted this LEO problem – and me probably – to go away as quickly as possible.

I laid out my case. LEO wanted a million. I knew they were never going to pay that but there's always a number people settle at. He got really nervy when I said I knew of six other firms lining up to lodge claims and perhaps I might be offering my services to them as well. PLUM was also probably shitting itself that this could leak out. It is an award-winning business and it didn't need to turn itself into the BHS of the building world.

PLUM's man played his card. There were problems with LEO, he claimed, so the million is a non-starter, which I already knew. Here was the offer – £150k upfront and another £350k worth of work over the next 18 months. And as a little sweetener for me, an extra £20k on the side if I left the other six companies to sort their own mess out.

Fuck me, only been here half an hour and I already had 70 grand coming my way! Happy fucking days all round as far as I was concerned and we shook on the deal. I could take this one to the bank 'cos I can't imagine LEO turning its back on this as it put them right back in the game.

All that was left to be done was for PLUM's CEO to sign off on the deal along with my client and the job's a good 'un. I'm so confident it's in the bag I take off on holiday for a couple of weeks. Why not? When the papers are signed, there were 70 large ones going into my bank account.

Fucking holiday. Big mistake. Turned my back for one minute and what happened? It all went fucking tits up.

Turns out my lad at LEO took it upon himself to see if he could pull off a better deal than the one I shook hands on. Stupidly, he went down to London and, with a big bevvy on board, met the guy from PLUM at his office and asked for £200k upfront along with three years of guaranteed work. No fucking chance.

'Cos I'm away in Portugal I knew fuck all about any of this until I got back from me hollies and am back in the office when the lad from PLUM was on the phone and told me what had gone down. Fucking prick is all I thought. I could fucking kill the lad from LEO for fucking this up. I'm only half listening when the PLUM fella suddenly asked very nicely if I could pop down to see them in London and meet with their CEO. 'Course I fucking will, any chance to salvage something out of this I had to fucking jump at.

Next day I'm back at PLUM's offices and in walked the CEO. Nice guy, sound fella, you'd have read about him in the money pages not so long ago. Had a bonus last year that could choke a whale. He tried to make me feel all comfortable but I'd rather just get on with it.

"Look let's cut all the bullshit and just get down to it," I said. "I know what you want. You want to pay me and to just fuck LEO off."

"Well yes, in a nutshell," said the CEO.

"Well that ain't going to happen 'cos I don't work that way. That's just being a prick ain't it? You pay me and I fuck him off."

"Please let me explain, Shaun. He came in here full of alcohol demanding to see me, not drunk but ranting. He was shouting, 'Look at this place. I want fucking more money'. It's just not the way to behave in business. You know that. And I guess you don't know this bit of information either. The work LEO did for us required certificates signed off showing the job had been done to standard. We need these certificates but your client has kept them and it's holding up the entire project. He's now saying on top of all his other ridiculous demands he wants another £50,000 to return them. Shaun, you know we had a deal on the table that I would have signed off on but not now."

Shit, time for a rethink.

I just knew this guy was for real and I could tell that as things stood he was going to play hardball and there was no way they were paying LEO a penny. No money for LEO means I don't get me 50 grand fee. I asked for a piss break 'cos it gave me time to make a quick call to LEO to just triple check the CEO's story.

"You been down their offices shouting and screaming, doing 50 grand deals behind my back?" I asked him.

"Fuck 'em Shaun, they'll pay more, trust me," he said. "I've got them by the bollocks."

"Have you fuck, you prick. They were happy to pay for this to go away but now you're trying to play the big hard case and they won't be bullied. Listen, they'll tie you up in knots for years. You can't take on people like this. They'll come up with something fucking legal, that you were under-performing, late, whatever. I had a deal for you and now they are going to give you fuck all. You've gone behind my back and made me look like a right cunt. I was supposed to be advising, getting it sorted and you go in and ask for more.

"You've cost me money. They're not paying you, full stop. Not paying."

Silence at the other end as the penny dropped and he finally understood the position he'd put himself in.

"Shit Shaun, what do I do?"

"Not my fucking problem mate. They ain't playing any more and neither am I. End of."

Wash me hands and it was back in to see the CEO.

"Right, here's where we are up to," I told him. "I've lost the money LEO would have been paying me so I'm out of pocket big time. We've still got the handshake on the 20 grand if I stay away from the other firms who may come after you, correct? Well, I think we can all call it a day if there's a little bit on top of that. Okay?"

"Shaun, we can't be seen to be paying you anything related to LEO. If it gets back to LEO, we'd be screwed."

"Come on, just get one of your other subbies to pay me," I said, thinking on my feet. "You send them the cash, they pay me. Simple."

The CEO did a quick bit of thinking.

"Right, here's what I'll do. The tax on 20 grand is five, agreed? I'll pay you 25 grand by the end of the week and we're all settled. Agreed?"

Too fucking right it was agreed. I walked in here in danger of getting nothing. Where do I sign?

Couple of days later this Launa from some timber company I had never heard of rang asking for me bank account details so she could transfer the money over.

Bank balance looked great a few days later when I popped to the hole in the wall. Time for another holiday.

CHAPTER 17
THE GRAFTER

Normal sort of job. Dave, me mate, runs a second-hand car business where people who can't get a normal type of loan can do business. Dave's happy to provide a car so long as they can provide proof of their address and that they've got some regular money coming in. The log book, though, stays with him 'til the car's paid off.

Dave was bounced by some young scally who ran up a £2,800 debt on a blue Renault Laguna, so he called me in to get the payments back on track.

The lad, Tommy, lived out at Seaforth and it was the usual story when I knocked the door of his flat on this shitty, run-down estate. Me mate Steve came along for moral support, if you know what I mean.

Woman opened the door, not bad looking for once, and I asked if Tommy was in.

"Oh no, he's out working at the moment," she said.

"Out working is he?" I replied.

That's good to know 'cos if he's working he's earning and that means he's got money.

She immediately realised she'd put her foot in it and tried to make amends.

"No, not working, just running around doing a few errands."

"Okay love, when he comes back can you get him to bell us 'cos I need to talk to him? You his wife? You could bell him now and I could talk to him – it's about the car."

"Oh yeah, I know about that. He's spoken to Dave and it's sorted."

"No it ain't love, that's why I'm here. Dave's sent me to sort it. Your man owes 2,800 quid and we need a chunk paying off it."

"Hang on, I'll ring him."

She went inside the flat leaving Steve and me on the doorstep.

A couple of minutes later she's back and hands me her mobile. Tommy's on the other end.

"Hello mate, is it about that car?" Tommy said. "Look I'm going to start paying it back, £50 a month, honest."

"No, £50 a month is not good enough mate. At that rate, it'll take ya four and half fucking years. Got to do better than that son."

"Look, I've only just got back to work…"

"Work? Your bird said you weren't working, just out doing errands."

"Not *work*, work, grafting, only got me round back last week."

Now I don't know what they call it where you live but grafting where I live means dealing. Our Tommy, it turned out, pushed coke, pills and anything he could get his hands on to the local druggies. Fair enough, where there was a demand someone will always supply and so long as he settled up with Dave, what had it got to do with me how he earned his living?

"So if you're grafting lad you can pay me, can't ya?"

"No mate, I've only just got back at it, there's no money yet. Can ya give me a couple of weeks to get meself sorted?"

"No, I need to see you now lad. I need some money today."

"Fuck, all right, give me a few minutes and I'll be there."

Sure enough, he was back at the flat not long after and had £200.

"Right lad, that'll do for starters. Now you need to start making your payments on time with Dave and I'll be back in two weeks when you'd better have £500 for me so you can catch up on what you owe. So get grafting lad, okay?"

"No problem, promise ya I'll have it."

Fortnight later I should have known – give someone a break and they'll always let you down. I'm too soft by half, me.

Dave didn't hear a word out of the little prick, he didn't make his due payment and I was back on the job.

I had a mobile number for Tommy so gave him a ring and he began his sob story.

"Sorry Shaun, honest, I've not been out so there's been no money coming in. Swear to ya, Shaun. If I had it, I'd pay it. Give me a couple more weeks and I'll have it."

I could just tell down the phone he was feeding me a load of bullshit and to make sure I was right I asked around with some of the lads I knew who were into coke whether they had heard of a new grafter out in Seaforth.

Sure enough, it didn't take long before the answer came in – there was a new lad called Tommy on the scene and his coke was top drawer with people queueing round the block to buy.

Tony, a mate in my gym, explained what was going on.

"Tommy's stuff is the biz Shaun," he said. "And he's always available whatever time of day – that's his promise. Three for a nifty too, fucking cheap."

And luckily for me, Tony had the number of Tommy's graft phone – the one he used for work.

The piss-taking little twat. Not earning any money, eh? Time to pay him a visit.

Saturday night I drove out to Seaforth taking Tony with me. The plan was that Tony would ring him asking for a score and then Tommy would drive to us to make the sale. Of course, it won't just be Tony waiting for him when he arrived. Simple really.

Tony made the call and he answered straight away. He told him what he was after and Tommy told him the price and where they should meet to do the deal. Sure enough, within 15 minutes Tommy pulled into the car park of The Railway pub in Seaforth and went straight into the boozer to do his deal with Tony. Seven for a one-r, special Saturday-night offer. I waited in the car park and as soon as Tommy went into the pub, I was out of my car and straight over to the Laguna, opened the door and jumped in. Happy days, keys were in the ignition and on the passenger seat was Tommy's 'graft phone', which was a massive bonus. I could pass that on to some of the grafters I knew, they would pay a decent price for the business they would be picking up from Tommy's customers.

I just slipped the phone into my pocket when I spotted Tommy walking out of the pub. He headed straight back to his car. His fucking face was a picture when he pulled open the door and saw me sitting behind the wheel.

"You, ya little shit, no fucking money? Time to pay up lad," I said.

You would have thought he would have done a runner, but Tony only gave him a couple of seconds before he followed him outside. Tommy wasn't going anywhere but I couldn't believe it when he started up with the same old bullshit that he didn't have any money.

"Shaun, Shaun, honest I ain't got it, I ain't been working," he protested.

"Not working you prick? You've just nicked 100 quid off my mate, Tony. 'Course you've got it."

I jumped out of the car and Tommy stood trembling as I got him to empty his pockets. Surprise, surprise, as Cilla used to say – just short of a grand. And a little Brucie Bonus – 16 bags of beak which I could pass on to one of me mates 'cos I don't touch the stuff.

"No fucking money you little shit. I'll have that. Now you can fuck off 'cos the car's going back too. Fucking walk home."

What could he do? He wasn't paying, couldn't call the cops 'cos someone's nicked his dosh – how's a little scrote like him going to explain having a fucking grand in cash? The bizzies ain't stupid.

Time to head home, so I jumped into the Laguna, out of the car park and onto the road. I was not half a mile away when there was a blue light in me mirror. The fucking bizzies.

Jesus, this was not looking pretty. I had near enough a grand in cash, 16 bags of coke and a mobile phone with a million different numbers and texts from druggies who were ringing Tommy for their gear. Shit.

There was a copper at me window so I wound it down and took a deep breath.

"Excuse me sir, we've just had this car reported stolen from The Railway pub car park," he said. "Could you step out please?"

"Hold on mate, who reported it stolen?"

"It was an anonymous call, sir, we just happened to be driving by when the call came in. So, could you step out of the car please."

Fucking Tommy – the little prick had done me up like a fucking kipper. If I was searched, I was seriously fucked. On top of that the fucking graft phone was buzzing away. Fucking hell, he must have been making a fortune the rate the texts are coming in.

"Honestly officer, this ain't been stolen," I said, thinking quickly. "It's been repossessed – the lad who's called ya hasn't been making the repayments and the leasing company have asked me to recover it."

Thank God Dave did this side of the business properly 'cos if you remember, all the paperwork stayed with him 'til the loan is paid off.

"If you run the number plate officer, you'll see it's owned by a leasing company," I told him.

Buzz, buzz, the phone was going again – more bloody deals coming through.

"Officer, you can ring the leasing company and check with them. Here's the number," and I gave him Dave's mobile.

"Wait there sir, I'll be back in a moment," he said.

He was about to walk off and ring Dave when who walked down the road? Fucking Tommy!

"Hey lad, got ya have they? Been grafting hard?" he shouted, pissing himself at the idea I was about to get lifted big time.

Tommy's shouting got the bizzies' attention 'cos they aren't stupid. They know what grafting is and they know what's going on when a mobile's ringing as much as the one in my pocket, especially when I'm not fucking answering it.

The officer was back at the door.

"Was there anything in the car when you got in it, sir?" he asked.

Quick, think.

"Oh yeah, there was this phone on the floor on the passenger side," I replied. "That's why I ain't been answering it 'cos it ain't mine. Here's my phone," I said, and produced me own mobile out my jacket pocket.

"Anything else, sir?"

"No, haven't looked in the boot or anything, just got behind the wheel and drove off."

"Let's take a look together sir," said the bizzie and we walked round to the boot and he opened it up. Fucking hell – a set of scales and dozens of little plastic bags.

I thought I was getting fucking nicked here. This looked bad.

"Mate, that's got fuck all to do with me, honest. Look, ring the lad whose number I gave ya. He'll tell ya I'm just picking up a car for him."

"Just stay there please sir," said the bizzie who walked off and talked to his partner. Should they just lift me straight away or make the call? My heart's pumping when at last the bizzie pulls his own phone out and makes the call.

Please God, Dave, answer the fucking phone and get this right.

It was a very fucking long five minutes before the bizzie came back.

"Right Sir, we've spoken to your company and they've confirmed you're working for them. I'm afraid, though, we're going to have to confiscate the car 'cos as I'm sure you'll agree it clearly looks like someone's been using it for dealing in drugs. Can we give you a lift?"

A lift? Fucking hell if he knew what was in my pockets he wouldn't be offering me a lift home, just a fucking drive to the nick.

"It's all right officer, I'll ring a mate who lives local and he can pick me up."

Tony was going to be nearby wondering what's happened to me.

I was off down the road as soon as I handed the keys over to the coppers, warmed up by the thought of soon catching up with that little shitbag Tommy and what I was going to do to him.

Fortunately for him, when the bizzies rang Dave he'd told them who the car was leased to. Even before I'd got home, the police had kicked his front door in. Lying on the kitchen table was £7,500 in cash and a mountain of coke.

Now, if only he hadn't been so cocky and paid up the money he owed for the Laguna, he wouldn't have ended up with a five-year stretch inside.

Fucking wanker.

CHAPTER 18
THE VAN

A couple of summers ago, I took the car into me mate Andy's garage for some work on the engine. It was going to take a few days to fix so Andy said I could take me pick from whatever was on the forecourt and borrow it for a few days.

There was only one thing I wanted – a black transit with Private Ambulance written down the side. I could have some fun with that, I thought.

Andy was not keen 'cos he picked up this coffin carrier for a bargain price and was going to strip the coffin gear out, refurb the inside and sell it on for a healthy profit.

"You can have it for the weekend, but I want it back without a scratch," he said.

"No problem, Andy, you know you can trust me," I said.

An hour later I was back at me pub and parked it up round the back. I went inside and saw Danny, one of me regulars.

"Come here Dan lad, do us a favour," I asked him.

Dan put his pint down and came out the back.

"Quick, get in the back and pull that sheet over ya. When you hear me come back, make out like Lazarus, okay?"

Back into the bar and there was a group of me mates chatting away – usual bollocks about footie which, unlike most Scousers, I don't give a fuck about.

"Hey lads, wanna see this fucking motor I've just got?" I told them. "Fuckin' bargain. Come and have a look."

We all walked to the back of the pub, pints in hand and I guessed they thought I'd bought a new Porsche or something, the fuss I was making.

"What the fuck are you going do with that, Shaun?" shouted one of the lads when they clocked eyes on the van. "It's a fucking hearse."

"It's not a hearse, you prick, it's a Private Ambulance. Only cost me a few grand. I'm going to leave the sign on 'cos no bizzies are ever going to pull over one of these."

"Here, open the back lad, let's have a look," said Titch. He's nicknamed that 'cos he's about 6ft 5in.

I got the keys and unlocked the door.

"Fucking hell Shaun, you prick, there's a fucking body still in it. Fucking hell lad."

"No fucking way," I said, playing it up big time.

"You're fucking right. Jesus, what the fuck? Here, grab those handles and we'll pull it out. Maybe we'll know who it is."

"No fucking way, it's fucking dead. Leave it out."

"Don't be a pussy, just grab the handles and pull. Ready, one, two, three."

And as it slid back Danny, right on cue, suddenly sat up on the trolley.

Ever heard five grown men scream? Fucking brilliant. Me and Dan were pissing ourselves all fucking day.

Must have pulled this gag all over the weekend and it worked a dream every time. Great fun.

Monday morning the phone went and it was Andy, apologising 'cos me car's not ready. It needed a part that wouldn't be in 'til the end of the week.

"You all right keeping with the van 'til then? It's still in one piece ain't it?" he asked.

"Sure, it's fine and I'm having a blast mate. See ya Friday."

The next day it was a scorcher, and I was outside the pub with two of me mates. One's a really close pal, Mark, sound lad and a bit of a "name" in the city. Jerry's the other. Both a right laugh. Andy's van was parked just a few yards away at the side of the road.

We were just shooting the breeze when down the street I saw this gold MS4 Lexus coming along. Bit odd, it was going about the speed of a milk float. As it passed the pub, I could see three lads in the back, two in the front. Me alarm bell's immediately going off big time 'cos you don't get a big car like that full of juice heads without someone heading for trouble. Someone's getting it.

The Lexus drove about 50 yards past the pub, did a U-turn and headed back our way.

"Fuck it lads," I shouted to Mark and Jerry, "It's going off here."

Sure enough, the Lexus drove towards us and then slowed to a stop.

"Ee are, lads, they want it, these, get ready," I shouted.

One of the lads in the car got out, fucking big muscle head. He ain't asking for directions.

"You want it, you cunt. Come on then," I shouted. I've never been backwards in coming forward as you know.

As I walked towards him, the passenger door on the Lexus suddenly opened and there was an arm pointing straight at the lads and me.

Boom, boom, boom.

Fucking shit! The cunt was fucking shooting at us!

I was dodging like shit to get out of the way – weaving this way and that like I was in the fucking SAS.

Get inside the pub, that's all I could think, and that's exactly what Mark and Jerry were doing. I could see them diving through the door.

Boom. Boom.

The cunt was still fucking firing.

I got to the door – and it was fucking locked!

Me fucking mates locked me out, the fucking bastards.

Boom. Boom.

Shit! Only one thing for it, charge the bastards. There were some empty beer bottles lying on the floor so I grabbed them and then ran straight at the Lexus, hurling the bottles like fucking bombs straight at the shooter and his mates.

Thank fuck the sight of this maniac running straight at them after all the shots they'd fired was enough to persuade them they'd better head for the hills. Fuck knows what would have gone down had I managed to catch up with the Lexus before it sped off down the road.

Time to catch my breath. Jesus. What the fuck was that all about?

I was fucking raging. Someone had tried to fucking kill me and to make it even worse me mates locked me out of my own pub.

"Open the fucking door, ya twats, open it," I shouted.

I'm kicking and shoving it 'til it swung open and one of the barmen was standing there.

Fucking Mark and Jerry were hiding in the loo at the back of the pub.

"You okay?" said Mark when he and Jerry emerged a few seconds later.

"Okay, you fucking twat, yez locked me out, left me fucking out there fucking getting shot at."

Now Mark's a bright lad, quick on his feet.

"Locked yer out, what yer on about? Jerry, did you fucking lock the door you twat?" And with that he landed a bell-ringer round his ear. Mark fucking knew the door was locked but he was covering his arse and Jerry knew he wasn't going to argue the point.

Fuck it, I'm in one piece, I'll leave it.

I stepped outside and that was when I noticed the van.

Seven shots I counted and not one of them hit me or the lads. The van, though, was a different story. It looked like a piece of Swiss cheese, holes fucking everywhere. Andy was not going to be happy.

I was just taking this in when the first bizzies arrived and soon they were swarming all over the place searching for the Lexus, helicopter buzzing overhead, but it was long gone.

They wanted to question us of course and all we could tell them was exactly what went down. Seven shots, five in the car and absolutely no fucking idea what it was about. I'd find out, but that came later.

There were forensic people all over the place and the van was the star attraction. Couple of hours later it was on the back of a police trailer and off to a lab to see if it could throw up any clues to the shooter.

Next morning Andy was on the phone and it was immediately obvious he hadn't heard about yesterday's events.

"Hey lad, car's ready. You can come round anytime this morning with the van and pick it up. Okay?"

Shit. The bizzies told me it would be with them for a few days and after that I would have to see if I could get the thing repaired.

"Listen, Andy, if it's all right with you can I keep it 'til the end of the week? I've got a couple of jobs on where the van's going to be really useful."

"Sure Shaun, anything you want, just keep any scratches off it, okay. Bring it back on Monday and if I'm not there just drop the keys in the office."

Scratches! What about the fucking bullet holes?

I'm thinking, okay, pick it up from the bizzies on Friday and I could drop it off at me mate John's garage where he could get to work fixing it up. Should be a piece of piss.

But when I picked it up you should have seen it. Seven bullet holes, yeah, but they were the size of fucking saucers. The whole thing was also smothered in forensic powder, bits of tape, handprints everywhere. A fucking mess. Andy was going to go fucking nuts.

I took a few photos of the bullet holes on me mobile phone and sent them to John at his garage 'cos there's no point taking the van there if he ain't going to be able to fix the damage.

He was on the phone straight away.

"Fucking hell Shaun, I can't. Little bullet holes yeah but not these. What did they use? A fucking tank? Listen, mate, just give it back, it's absolutely fucked."

Well, we Scousers are supposed to have a great sense of humour. Maybe Andy would see the funny side so I gave him a call.

"Andy, you about, going to bring the van back now, okay?"

"Sure. Hey, I hear you've had a bit of bother? What happened, you okay?"

"Yeah, fucking hell mate, never better. I'll tell yer about it when I see yer."

"So long as you're okay Shaun, that's the main thing."

Glad he saw it that way. Wait 'til he sees his motor.

Thank fuck when I got to his yard I was able to park it up without him seeing me. Tucked it up behind another van so he could only see the front, not all the forensic shit and the fucking holes.

As I walked over to his office with the keys, Andy spotted me through the window and walked out to meet me.

"Everything all right Shaun? Good to see yer," he said.

"Fine, sound. Look here's a one-r for the van, for the extra week, like."

"Don't be a twat Shaun. I don't want your money."

"Take it mate, you might need it."

"I don't want your one-r, we're mates."

"Listen take it, you'll need it."

"What for?"

"I don't know, buy the kids some sweets or something. Here, take it."

I handed him the money and headed off, shouting back 'Speak to you in a bit then'."

"Why, what's up. There's something up with you, what is it?"

"Nuttin, speak to yer later."

A mate was waiting to give me a lift back to the pub and we had not gone 100 yards down the road when Andy's on the phone.

"What the fucking hell has happened to me van you fucking crazy cunt? You cheeky bastard, get back here."

He was raging but I pissed myself laughing so we span back to his yard and there was Andy, head in his hands shouting at his lads.

"Look at the fucking thing! Look at it you stupid bastards."

"Hey Andy, what's up?"

"What yer doing? What yer doing? Look at the fucking van. It's going to cost me a bloody fortune."

"Hang on, that's what the one-r was for. Come on mate."

"Come on mate! Fucking mate. This is going to cost me a fucking fortune."

"Hang on, what about this morning? I thought it was 'So long as you're okay' that was the most important thing?"

"That was before I saw me fucking van, Shaun."

"Listen, I'm safe, they never got me, just yer van as it happens.

Look mate, I'm just taking the piss, 'course I'll pay for it. See the funny side, will ya."

"Shaun, you are fucking nuts. I knew it was a fucking bad move giving you the van – you could have been shot and be laying out in one of these. I'm never lending you a fucking car ever again."

To be honest the bill he gave me was a cheap price to pay given how things could have gone.

Fucking funny with the Lazarus gag, though.

CHAPTER 19
THE AFFAIR

Oone thing I have learned in life is you never know when shit's going to happen. It just does and there's only one thing you can do about it and that's try and deal with it.

Phone goes one day at the office and there's this guy, Trevor, desperate to make an appointment to see me. He turned up, suited and booted and seemed a really nice, smart lad. He told me he owned an IT company with about 20 employees that was turning over a couple of million a year. He was married with a couple of kids, had a house worth £800,000 and his mortgage was paid off. Lovely, wouldn't mind a slice of that myself.

"So what's the problem mate?" I asked him.

Turns out he and his wife were selling the house and she wanted to put all the money into a new joint bank account.

"Something's wrong," he said. "Any money we've had has always gone into my account. I handle everything. Something's not right."

No shit Sherlock, she's playing away. You can smell this from a million fucking miles away.

"I don't care what it costs, I want you to follow her and see what's going on," said Trevor.

Dead easy job, £250 a day and exes – I'll knock this one out myself, no need to have anyone riding shotgun. For a week I was her shadow. I tailed her to the gym, Tesco, the hairdresser and nail salon. Wherever she moved, I was on her tail. When she was at home, I parked just over the road and watched everyone who knocked the door – from the postman to the carpet fitter and the gas man.

On the face of it, she didn't put a foot wrong, so after a couple of weeks I got Trev back in my office and gave him my report.

"There's nothing there mate," I told him. "I can keep on it but it's costing you money. Your choice."

He was convinced there was something wrong but decided to leave it. His call, not mine. Six weeks later he was back and like a totally different man. His suit was all crumpled and he was a bag of nerves – all over the place, bottle of brandy tucked into his jacket pocket. I needed to calm him down and find out what happened.

I asked Terry, a lad who worked with me in my office, to put the kettle on and fetch us some Wagon Wheels. Blue Riband, Wagon Wheels and two-finger Kit Kats are me favourite biscuits. If I give you a Wagon Wheel, you're me mate, I like ya. Trevor brought me up to date.

Even though I hadn't spotted it, his missus was playing away – with the fucking carpet fitter! He'd only been in the house less than 15 minutes so I'd ruled him out. If he was giving her one while I was outside, it must have been fucking quick. And to make matters worse, to me anyway, he's an ex-screw.

How did he find out, I asked him?

"Look Shaun, I'm not fucking thick," he said. "When you get a carpet fitted, you may call the fitter back once or twice but it suddenly dawned on me he was there twice a week every fucking week. He was fitting something – my fucking wife."

Trev's story got worse 'cos as soon as he found out she was playing away, she fucked off back to her mother's. He was right not to open a joint account 'cos before she fucked off to stay at her mum's, she nicked his bank details and transferred £100,000 into her own private account.

"Here's what I want you to do, Shaun. I've got plenty of money. I'll pay whatever you want – I want him to go missing," he said.

"You what?" I replied. "Don't be a cunt, Trevor. You want me to make him go missing? As in missing? You're asking the wrong guy, mate. This is real life, not the fucking telly."

"Shaun, please. I want him to go missing. I want you to kill him. I want her back."

"Listen Trev, I ain't killing fucking no-one."

"Shaun I've got £800,000 in the house, you can have it."

"I don't care how much you've got it ain't happening. I really, really can't. Look, Trev, all I can do is go and warn this guy off and warn your bird off him, too. If she gets back with you that's down to her. Take it or leave it."

Trev's got no choice really. I ain't killing the bloke so he settled for me scaring him off his missus. So a couple of days later I borrowed one of me mate's flats and got me bird to call the carpet fitter to come round and price a job. He came walking in like a cocky fucker.

The flat's brand new, sparkling with a lovely parquet floor.

"Hey mate, you don't want to be putting carpet on this stuff," he said.

"Yes I do and I want it like this one," I said and handed over a photo. "You might recognise it – it's the carpet from me mate's bedroom where you've been shagging his fucking wife."

He looked at the photo and his arse fell out of his trousers quicker than they'd fallen round his knees when he was popping round to screw her.

"Here's what's going to happen," I said. "We're going to have a conversation and you need to listen. You are going to ring her up and tell her it's over and if you don't, I'll roll you up in your own carpet and we'll see if you can swim the Mersey. I'm not fucking about, this is serious."

Trevor's wife was ready to give up everything – perfect home, kids and money in the bank – because she thought she found true love. And she fucked it all up. This fucker wasn't in love and didn't give two fucking hoots about her. He was just after a shag.

"I don't want any trouble mate," he said. "Give us your phone and I'll call her."

And he did it right there in front of me – no quiet chat over a coffee holding hands and saying goodbye.

"It's over," he said. "It's going nowhere. It's just been sex. Don't contact me again."

And he put the phone down. Pretty brutal, but job done.

"That do ya?" he said. "Was getting boring anyway and the sex wasn't up to much."

Fuck him. The state Trevor got himself into and this twat didn't give a fuck about any of it. If Trevor were here, he'd have given him a good slap so, fuck it, I did it for him.

Trevor's wife took 48 hours to come to her senses and went back home.

Funny that – stay at her mum's or back to that lovely big house, her kids and the good life.

A couple of months later Trevor dropped by the office. He was wearing jeans and an open shirt and looked brand new.

"I've never been so happy, everything's great," he told me. "We've bought a little villa abroad. It's like it never happened and I owe it all to you. When I came in to see you, I was fucked. I really wanted that guy killed. I am so happy I took your advice. Can I give you a hug?"

"No you fucking can't, you big girl," I told him.

"All right, can I buy you a Wagon Wheel then?"

"Now you're talking."

CHAPTER 20
THE CARAVAN

I took this job one time in Burnley – God knows why 'cos what a shithole that place is. Can't think why anyone in their right mind would want to live there.

This guy, Ray, had called me because he had a spot of bother with some local building developers who'd bought some land off him. Ray laid out the story when I met him in a café and on the face of it the job seemed simple enough.

Ray had been left a plot of land by his dad, which he'd sat on for seven years while it increased in value. When the time was right, he stuck in an application for outline planning permission to put houses on the site and, sure enough, it sailed through and got the green light. In just a few weeks, he found these buyers who met the asking price of £400,000 and after all the paperwork had gone through, they gave him a month to remove anything he owned from the site.

This is where he'd come a bit unstuck 'cos all over the plot – which used to be an old textile factory – was a mountain of scrap metal. For the few weeks he had left, Ray worked round the clock with a couple of mates to take away as many old bits of steel and copper as he could find. He even stayed on the site in this luxury caravan he owned, which he normally used for touring round the continent.

And it turns out the caravan was the problem. On the day he was supposed to vacate, he took a load of scrap off to a dealer's yard but when he returned, the gates to the site were padlocked and his caravan was stuck inside.

"It's worth at least 30 grand, Shaun," he explained.

"I thought it was just a mistake but when I rang the buyers they just told me to fuck off and read the contract. Sure it said I had until that day to take off the site anything I wanted, but this was just taking the piss. I've tried reasoning with them but they're just not listening."

Now, he just put 400 large ones into his bank account so he could have easily afforded to go out and buy himself a new toy, so why bother with all this hassle? He would also have to pay me a whack to help him get it back.

"Shaun, I just don't like people who play like this. They're just bloody bullies who think they can get away with anything they want. I've asked around and everyone says this is just the sort of thing you can sort out."

Indeed it is and I was happy to take his money especially as it had been a bit quiet and the old bank balance wasn't looking that healthy.

"Sure, I can sort this out but it's going to cost you 10 grand, okay?" I said.

"No problem," he replied.

"Right, tell me about the people you've been dealing with. Who's in charge?"

"Well, the people who bought the land off me are two brothers from Albania, the Bardhis."

Shit, he could have fucking mentioned a lot bloody sooner that we were dealing with a bunch of fucking Albanians! Only ones I know with any decent money are fucking gangsters and not the easiest people to deal with.

"Fucking hell mate, thanks for telling me. No wonder you can't fucking sort this yerself."

Still, there was some decent money on the table and I have never been one to turn down a job just 'cos there might be spot of bother down the line.

Next day I was back down the M65 to go and pay the Bardhis

a visit. Normally I'd just have brought a mate along with me, headed straight to the site, blagged my way on, hooked up the caravan and offski. Better this time, I thought, to knock the door first and see if I can reason with them.

For people who've got some serious money to throw around, the Bardhis certainly don't show it. When I walked into their office above a travel agent's in the centre of town, it looked more like a fucking waiting room at a taxi firm. The two brothers are the only people in the room and they look fucking hard. Both are well over 6ft and look like they've spent most of their lives in the gym – fucking muscles everywhere. I can look after myself but I was pretty sure if this all kicked off I was going to be up against it. Better play it cool.

I explained who I was and why I was there, and throughout there was not a fucking peep out of either of them. At the end of my talk, the three of us were just sat there staring at each other.

Some fucking game this, so finally I asked 'em: "Come on lads, what's it going to be? You going to let him have his van back or we going to fall out?"

"You go, Mr Smith," one of 'em piped up. "You make big mistake coming here. This not your business."

"Sorry mate, it is my fucking business. And if there's been any fucking mistake it's you fucking clowns not listening to me. You've tried to pull a fast one but it ain't happening."

"Mr Smith, you listen carefully. You make trouble for us we make very bad trouble for you, which you not like, understand? We make trouble for you and your whole family."

Now that's not very nice, no need to bring the family into this.

"Listen lads," I said, "you don't know who you're dealing with. Ask around, yous are just off the fucking boat and haven't got a fucking clue. I've been dealing with twats like you all me life and your silly threats don't fucking scare me.

"Now I've asked you nicely to give me man his van back and yous don't want to listen. Fair enough, we'll see what happens next then, won't we."

We were back to that fucking staring game for a minute, before I got up and walked back to the car. Well, that didn't go as well as I hoped for, did it?

No time to hang about on this job 'cos if I was the Albanians, I'd be having Ray's caravan off the site sharpish and he would probably never see it again. So, the next night I was back in Burnley with a couple of mates, and I borrowed a Rover 'cos it's got the tow bar we'll need to hitch on the caravan.

When we got to the site we couldn't believe our luck 'cos even though the gates were locked there was no nightwatchman and there was the fucking van parked right in the yard. Piece of piss.

The lock was gone in a jiffy and within a couple of minutes we had the van hooked up and were off down the road. Never had a job go so easy. These Albanians, fucking amateurs.

We drove the van back to Warrington and it was only when we parked up behind me gym that we heard it – there was fucking murders going on inside the caravan. It was rocking all over the fucking place. What the fuck is it?

"Here Titch, open the door and see what the fuck's going on will ya?" I said.

"Fuck off Shaun, you fucking do it. This ain't right."

"Fucking pussy, come on, let's have a look."

It was still rocking like crazy as I reached for the door handle and just as I was about to pull it down, there was this deep growl from inside. Fuck this, I thought, best look through the window

173

first and see what's going on.

Just as I put my face to the glass, I fucking shit meself when two fucking snarling rottweilers leapt straight at me. The fucking distance I jumped back I would have made the bloody Olympic long-jump team. No fucking nightwatchman? Didn't fucking need one with those crazy bastards inside.

The dogs were going even crazier now, barking like fuck, and you could hear them charging round inside. We were lucky the club was not near any houses 'cos the noise they were making would wake the fucking dead.

Fuck it, they could bark all fucking night for all I cared. I needed my bed.

The next day things didn't look a lot better. In fact it was a bloody nightmare.

The dogs seemed to be quiet when the lads and I walked up to the van but as soon as they could see me at the window they were off again, howling like bloody banshees. And inside the van, I could see it was a fucking disaster 'cos the rotties fucking ripped the place to bits. It may have been worth £30,000 yesterday but it wasn't now. The dogs were in there too long and nature took its course 'cos I could see where they were pissing. There were shitty paw prints everywhere, too.

Shit, if these fucking things are in there much longer, we might as well put a fucking match to the thing. Problem is how to get the dogs out without them ripping to pieces the first person through the door? Unless it was someone they knew who could control them, they could kill someone.

There was no choice. We would have to take our chances and take the fucking van back and dump it at the site. Let the fucking Albanians deal with it.

For the fourth time in a week, it was back to fucking Burnley where we got a piece of luck. The site was exactly as we left it the night before, gates wide open and no-one in sight. We were like a fucking Formula 1 tyre crew getting the caravan off the tow bar and parked back where it was. Time to go home. Wonder what the Bardhi boys will have to say about this.

In fact, it was not that much later when me phone went and it was one of the Albanians on the line.

"Mr Smith, how are you? I take it you are well," he said.

"What is it mate, what you after?"

"Listen Mr Smith, we have been asking about you to some of our friends and maybe we can do some business with you after all."

"I'm listening."

"I speak to my brother and we decide you can have the caravan back as you wanted but there is one problem."

"What's that then mate?"

"Well it seems someone took the van last night and did not know we keep our dogs inside. They are lovely animals but can get very angry when they are with people they don't know. I can understand why whoever took the van would bring it back."

"What sort of dogs are they mate?"

"Rottweilers Mr Smith, as I'm sure you remember."

Clever fucker, they've played it well here. Didn't think this Albanian had it in him.

"So what do we do now, mate?" I asked.

"You can pick the van up any time you like, tell your friend he can have it. Nice to do business with you."

Well, that didn't go too bad – whoever they spoke to must have put a good word in about me to make 'em so reasonable.

I'm straight on the phone to Ray and told him he could pick

his caravan up straight away. He was over the moon, but that wouldn't last when he finally saw the state of the thing inside.

"Fucking hell Shaun, it's ruined," he said. "It'll cost me thousands to get this all put right."

"That's your problem mate. You asked me to help get it back and that's what I've done. I had to lean on those guys really hard to persuade them to give it up. I put myself out on a limb for you 'cos I did my homework and they are really serious players. You've got a load of money in the bank, just fucking shell some of it out and stop moaning. And by the way, remember it's payment in 14 days for my services. Do you want me to email me bank details?"

CHAPTER 21
THE BROTHEL

In my game, you never turn a client away. As long as I'm playing within the law and the money I'm chasing is legitimately owed, I'll take the job on. I was in the office one morning reading the paper when the phone rang. It was Malcolm, an old mate of mine or, rather, more of an acquaintance. Now Malcolm is one of those guys who's got his fingers in pies all over the place. The Revenue haven't heard of him, but the bizzies have 'cos a lot of what he gets up to isn't entirely legit.

One of Malcolm's little businesses is a small brothel, or a brass shop as we call it in Scouse land. He's owned it for 20 years, and it's a great little earner. Each day there are four girls working from 8am–4pm, before another crew arrive for the night shift. Most of the time they're pretty much working flat-out, so with Malcolm earning off every punter who walks through the door, he's put away a fortune.

Not so long ago he would sort out any problems himself, but he's getting on a bit now so whenever anything serious springs up, he's on the phone to me. He got straight down to business and explained the problem.

"I've had this fella coming to me for a couple of years now, regular as clockwork," Malcolm explained. "He's got a few bob, turns up in a little Mercedes Sport every Tuesday afternoon and is in and out fairly sharpish. He only asks for a blow job so, for the girls, it's easy money. On Thursdays, he returns but this time asks for the full works.

"He's been coming for so long I've let him run up a £1,500 bill, and I was on the point of asking him to settle up when things turned a bit tasty. Turns out, like a lot of my punters, he's got a funny habit. In his case, he never takes his trousers off, just leaves than hanging round his ankles. Doesn't matter what he's there for, the trousers stay on.

Last week as he was finishing off with one of the girls, a fucking gun fell out of his trousers. The girl nearly shit herself 'cos the punters we deal with are usually just old men and husbands who ain't getting it at home anymore. Not fucking gangsters, Shaun.

"He said to the girl to keep her fucking mouth shut and that he was a dangerous man who would make her and all the other girls' lives hell if they told anyone he was walking around with a gun in his pocket. Shoved the gun right in her face just to show how hard he was, the prick.

"Problem now, Shaun, is the girls don't want him anywhere near the place in case he's some fucking maniac. You'd be doing me a huge favour if you could sort it. He's due here next Thursday – always gets in about two o'clock. Could you have a little word in his ear to settle his bill and fuck off? That's all I need mate. You can keep the money – I'm not fussed about that. But I need the girls back at work without worrying if he'll be the next punter through the door."

Of course I took the job, I would never let Malcolm down, but going up against someone I know will be armed is not run-of-the-mill stuff. I had to be careful on this one. Thursday came round, and I drove out to Malcolm's place in Wigan. I got there nice and early, so I could have a good look around and get the lay of the land. As ever I've got a mate, Ollie, riding shotgun. Always game for a laugh and a good man to have in your corner if the balloon goes up.

I knew about the brass house for years, but I had never been inside. Turns out it's on a small industrial estate. You wouldn't think anything of it from the outside – it's a normal, office-type building with a girl on the front desk. At the back of the building there are four little "units" where the business gets done.

The whole place is decorated nicely but, Christ, if you're doing the naughties, the walls are so thin everybody can hear what's going on.

As luck would have it, the girl on the desk, Mary, is an old mate from the pub and we were soon chatting away after I had my walk round to suss out the place.

"Malcolm left a message, Shaun, that if you and your friend fancy it, you can have a girl each for free while you're waiting," Mary says. "It's been a bit quiet this morning, so the girls are, well, you know, ready for some fun."

Me mate Ollie's face lit up like a fucking Roman candle.

"Don't mind if I do," he said. "Got plenty of time ain't we Shaun?"

"You do what you want mate. Think I'll just stay and have a chat with Mary here. Make sure you're back in an hour, no more, 'cos I want this to go down proper."

Ollie dashed straight off to the girls' lounge, made his choice and disappeared off to the unit furthest away from the front desk.

Mary and I were nattering away for a while when the phone rang. She took the call and after a couple of minutes hung up.

"That was Malcolm," said Mary. "He's asked me to say he'd like you to enjoy one of the girls 'cos you're doing him such a favour. The girls won't mind, Shaun."

"Come on Mary, you know me," I protested. "This ain't my scene, no way."

She looked at me for a few seconds and then leaned over the desk and whispered: "There's a camera in the room, Shaun. Malcolm was going to record you at it."

What? I was doing Malcolm a favour, going up against a fucking guy with a gun, and he was going to film me going at it

180

with a brass. What the fuck was he playing at? First, though, I had to deal with the punter. I would get me head round Malcolm's little game later on.

Ollie had his fun and was back with me in reception when, good as gold, the punter arrived outside in his little red Mercedes.

"Right Mary, stick him in the room with the fucking camera running. Me and Ollie will be next door. When he has picked his girl, you and the others go for a little walk. Give us about half an hour. It should all be over by then."

Ollie and I were in our unit watching through a crack in the door when the punter walked past with today's afternoon entertainment. He'd picked a good-looking black girl.

Now don't forget we could hear every fucking sound of what was going on next door. Normally, Ollie and I would have been pissing ourselves like schoolboys, but we had to remember there was a gun in there and, whatever went down, he wasn't going to be happy. We gave him about 15 minutes to get going then made our move.

Ollie barged in first with me right behind him. There was our guy bent over the girl who was on all fours. As we charged in he was, shall we say, like Lester Piggott going down the last few yards in the Derby. Horrible sight, especially when he, er, dismounted and "crossed the finishing line" right there in front of us.

"What the fuck," he screamed just as Ollie landed one right across his ear sending him crashing to the floor. Even as he fell, I moved forward and grabbed for his trousers which, as we'd been told, were still hanging round his ankles.

Get the gun, get the gun, is all I thought and, sure enough, there it was in his right-hand pocket. I checked his other pockets and found his wallet and keys for the Merc parked outside. Game over for this little prick.

Ollie gave him a little kick right in the knackers, which, given what he'd just been doing, had more than the usual effect. He was gagging, and holding himself trying to deaden the pain.

Meanwhile, the brass was as good as gold. Just grabbed her clothes, stepped over the guy and went off to get dressed in one of the other cubicles.

"Right you fucker. Get your fucking kegs on," I said.

"What's fucking going on?" begged the punter.

"Not so fucking tough now are you, lad? Should have stayed waving your dick in the girls' faces rather than a fucking gun, hard man."

I had a quick look at it and saw it was a two-bullet Derringer. You can do some serious damage if you're right up close, but it's not the sort of thing serious gangsters walk around with (so I'm told).

I point the little pistol at him and cock the trigger.

"Like scaring girls do ya? Get off on it do ya?" I shouted. "Where I come from we fucking shoot pricks like you."

He seriously shit himself. I wasn't sure how hard I was going to run this out.

"Now messing with the girls is bad enough but I'm told you're such a cheeky bastard you ain't even been paying. With today's little action I reckon that's five grand you owe the house."

"No fucking way," he said. "That's bullshit."

Fair enough – he wanted to argue.

"Ollie, take the Merc for a drive will ya," I said as I threw him the keys.

Ollie was straight out the door, and a minute later you could hear him drive off down the road.

"Okay tough guy, your call. Here's what you can do. You pay the money you owe, stay away from the place and you can get the car back. This little pea shooter is staying with me. Can't have children playing with dangerous toys, can we? Don't want to play this way, well, over to you.

"Oh, by the way, do you want your wallet back? Nice picture of your wife and kids, I presume. By the way, do ya see that little glass thing there, above the door? That's the lens from the camera which was filming you banging away that brass 20 minutes ago. Can get a copy for your missus if you want? What's your address? Should be on your driving licence. Here it is – 21 Churchill Drive. I can drop the film off any time."

His fucking face was a picture. I could tell the prospect of his missus finding out how he spent his afternoons twice a week was more terrifying than sitting opposite me. Game, set and match.

"Alright if I make a call?" he asked, so I passed him the phone from his jacket which was lying on a chair next to the bed.

Whoever he rang wasn't asking many questions, just taking down the instructions to get hold of five grand in cash and to bring it straight to him.

"Should take about half an hour," he told me.

"As long as you want mate. You ain't going anywhere 'til this is sorted."

I left him in the room and went back out to reception just as Mary and the other girls arrived back.

"Job done. He'll be gone in a bit, and you won't be seeing him again, trust me. And here, keep this little Derringer-thing just in case any of your other punters get a bit lippy. It'll save me having to come round again."

Shaun Smith

Half an hour later a car arrived and there was a lad there with the money.

"Car's round the back, keys in the ignition, just had it taken round the block while we had our little chat. Now do yourself a favour son and fuck off home. Make sure we don't meet again, okay?"

Not a bad afternoon's work. I was a hero to a bunch of brasses and had five grand in cash. Only issue now was fucking Malcolm. What the fuck was he playing at? Not sure how I was going to play this 'cos he had never let me down before. Do I front him up straight away, I thought, or let it ride for a while?

When Malcolm rang me later that afternoon, he was all over me on the phone.

"Cheers Shaun, knew I could fucking rely on you," he told me. "Seriously, anything I can do for you, just ask. Doesn't matter what it is I'm there for you."

Fuck it, I could have kicked off at the two-faced cunt but I decided to bide my time.

"Cheers Malcolm, always glad to help. Call me any time mate."

For the time being, I was happy to spend the little bit of money I earned on the job. Ollie got a decent cut, but not as much as he could have 'cos don't forget he got a free fuck on the job.

Couple of months down the line I was chilling in the office with me mate Terry when the phone rang and it was Malcolm.

"Hi Shaun, how are you mate, everything okay?" he said.

"Great mate, fucking sound," I replied, wondering what he was up to.

"Shaun, I've got some news lad. I'm retiring, calling it a day and heading off to Spain. Time to enjoy life son."

"Fucking hell Malcolm! After all these years. What about all your businesses? You can't just walk away."

184

"Of course not, Shaun. I've got buyers for most of them and the money I'm getting I'll never be able to spend. Look, Shaun, you've always been good to me. I'd like to do you a favour and give you the brass house. It's yours – the building, girls, punters. It's great money lad and it's not just the stuff you get from the girls turning tricks. Listen, a couple of years ago I had this camera put in the wall in one of the rooms. When the right punter comes in who you can see has got some money, turn the camera on and make a movie. Once you tell them you've got it and would the missus like a copy they pay through the fucking nose. Works a treat Shaun, like the fucking Golden Goose."

Yeah, would have worked a fucking treat on me, too, if I'd taken up the offer of a freebie. The cheek of him to think he would get away with that on me. No fucking chance.

Must be an age thing 'cos, even though Malcolm was bang out of order, I was pretty blown away by the idea he was gifting me a payday like this. Only problem is, as you know, this ain't my sort of gig.

"Thanks, Malcolm, I appreciate it, but it's not my style," I explained. "I've got me own stuff to do that keeps me busy enough. Why don't you let the girls have it? At the end of the day, they're the ones doing all the work, aren't they?"

"Fair enough Shaun, thought you'd say that but I had to give you the chance. You know me, I always play a straight hand."

No you fucking don't, I thought, but I let it slide.

Malcolm sold up a few months later but was still at it as he made his arrangement to head off to the sun. It transpired some of his business associates weren't on as friendly terms with him as I was. He was on to at least half a dozen lads I knew, borrowing large from all of them. 'Course they'd been happy to oblige 'cos

Malcolm had always been around, always would be and had never welched on a debt.

Last I heard, and that's 18 months ago, he fucked off with about £100,000 in total!

CHAPTER 22
THE DUVET MAN

There's a lad in the pool team at the pub, Kevin, who took me to one side to see if I could help him out with a little problem. Nice lad Kev, always up for a laugh and, as far as I knew, never been in any bother.

I led him into the back office, put the kettle on and sat him down to hear his story. Kev's a real grafter, set up his company a few years back and was doing pretty well. Not sure exactly what it was he did, but it was something to do with bedding, quilts and pillows. Other than helping to change the sheets at home every other week, I leave all that sort of stuff to the missus. Kev was doing well, he told me, and made a decent bit of money – but then he got in bed with the wrong man.

"Suppose I was a bit greedy," said Kev. "This firm in Preston approached me with what looked like a fantastic opportunity. The company wanted to place a huge, 50 grand order with me, which is way above what I usually handle, and were looking for top-quality duvets, which is the stuff I make. I bring in all the materials from Egypt, make 'em up at my factory and then pass them on to whoever's placed the order. The customers then put their own branding on and sell them on the high street.

"Problem I had was taking on this job meant going to the limit of what I could borrow from the bank to get all the materials shipped in. Had to go down on my knees to persuade them to give me the money, but at the end of the day, they did play ball. It took nearly six weeks to complete the work, and I had to take on a couple of extra girls to make sure we hit the deadline, which we just managed to do.

"Last month I took everything up to the customer's place in Preston. The two guys I dealt with were as nice as pie when I was up there and said what a brilliant job I did. They even promised me more orders in the future. I came back thinking I cracked it 'cos with four or five orders like this a year I'd be rolling in it."

I took a sip of my tea at this point 'cos I fucking knew what was coming next.

"More fool me, Shaun. That's the last I've fucking heard from them. I expected them to pay me within 14 days of delivery, but there's been nothing. I have spent the last month trying to track 'em down, but their numbers just ring out. Been up to Preston half a dozen times, too, but their place is all locked up.

"I'm in the shit, Shaun. The bank's ringing 'cos I'm already missing some payments on the money I borrowed. The wife's fucking moaning every minute of the day that I didn't do me homework and should have known it was too good to be true. Fucking great, hey? Didn't fucking say that when she was out spending like it was going out of fashion, thinking the money was already in the bank.

"Come on Shaun, can you help? I need to find these fellas pretty sharpish and see if I can get some money back otherwise it's game over."

'Course I could help. I would never let one of me regulars down. And because he was 50 grand in the hole, there was going to be a decent pay day at the end of it if I could sort things out. First off I needed the basics of who I was looking for.

"They're two Irish brothers: John and Ryan McGreevey," Kev explained. "They're both well over 6ft, and when I went up to their offices, they had matching Range Rovers in the car park with personalised number plates, JM1 and RM1. That any use to you?"

You bet it was 'cos there's a lad I know who's a computer whizz and it wouldn't take him a minute to track 'em down.

Sure enough, the next day I was up at the crack of down

and off down the M6 to an address for brother John in this little village called Eccleshall just south of Stoke-on-Trent. If there was no-one home, I even had the other lad Ryan's address, which is just a bit further south in Stafford. The plan was first to see if there was anyone there and then second to find out where they were working from 'cos the size of the order meant they surely had a warehouse.

For once me luck was in 'cos parked outside the house was the Rover, just as Kevin described, with JM1 on the plate.

I was there for an hour, but there wasn't any sign of life. Then something happened. What must be one of his kids jumped into a baby BMW and raced off down the road. What is it about young lads when they're behind the wheel? It must have taken him a 100 yards to find second gear.

The lad I was after was next out, and it turned out he was a big fucker who looked like he could handle himself. He was into the Rover and off down the road with me a couple of hundred yards behind. I took the precaution of taking the missus' car that morning 'cos it could have looked a bit odd having two black Rovers following each other down country lanes.

We drove for about 20 minutes heading down towards Stafford when his car pulled off the main road into one of those new industrial estates. Excellent, straight to his office. I parked up and walked to see which building he was in.

There was a burger van parked up nearby, so I grabbed a cup of tea and went for me stroll. Round a couple of corners and there was JM1 right outside this huge warehouse, and it had RM1 right alongside. Luck was definitely in this morning. It was time for a chat with the brothers, but before I did, I decided to have a quick look inside the warehouse to see who was at home.

I crept round the back of the building and went in through the fire door. The fucking place was huge with row after row of shelving, all packed with cardboard boxes. Now, I wondered, what was inside these? As quietly as I could, I pulled one of the boxes off the shelf nearest me, ran me car key along the sealing tape and looked inside. Sure enough, it was packed with duvet after duvet. All top-of-the-range stuff exactly like Kevin made. His stuff had to be in there somewhere.

Enough of the detective stuff, I thought, let's go and have a chat with the boys.

There were some stairs at the side of the building that led up to a couple of offices overlooking the warehouse. No time like the present, so I was straight upstairs and through the door to where the brothers were.

"Morning gentlemen, got time for a chat?" I said, calmly.

They both looked up, wondering how the fuck I'd just wandered right into their office.

"Excuse me, how did you get in here?" said the one I'd followed to work, John.

"Through the fucking door mate. How the fuck else?"

Nothing like a bit of rich language to get someone's attention. They had to be thinking, "Who the fuck is this Scouser and what does he want?"

"Well, you shouldn't be up here. If you've business, you should be making an appointment, not just barging in," piped up the other lad, Ryan.

"Nah, thought I'd be better just dropping in like 'cos I hear you ain't too good at answering the phone."

"What the fuck does that mean? 'Course we answer the phone," said John.

"Fucking didn't when my mate Kevin was trying to ring yez. Been trying to get hold of you for a fucking month now 'cos he's a bit short of cash. But of course, yez know that don't ya? He's having a hard time of it since you fuckers were on yer toes out of Preston. Took all the stuff he supplied without paying and left him right up shit street."

It was Ryan's turn to speak.

"Sorry pal, that's life. Business went tits up overnight and there's nothing we could do. Lots of little fellas like yer mate Kevin lost out, and we lost a fortune ourselves. Company's gone into administration and anything that was worth anything got sold off to pay the Revenue. Fuck all left, sorry."

What a load of bollocks.

"Listen, mate, do I look fucking thick? My lad's stuff is downstairs in your fucking warehouse and by the looks of things he's not alone in having the rug pulled from under him. Do yourselves a favour and be good boys now and behave. I'd suggest a cheque to cover the money you owe, and I'll leave it at that. Okay?"

They were both out of their chairs now and walked towards me. Big lads the both of them. Perhaps would have been better not to fly solo on this one.

"Got a fucking pair on you, ain't ya?" said John. "Now we ain't writing a cheque for you or fucking anyone. Yer mate's just had a bit of bad luck, and he's going to have to live with it. Now listen carefully fella – you've been a big boy and done your job, but we're not the sort of people you should be messing with, understood? Carry on playing the hard man, and we'll be making your life very unpleasant."

Hard man, me? Never. I thought I could probably take the two of these if it came to it, but it would be a pretty close thing.

Time to make a strategic withdrawal.

"All right lads, I understand. Just doing my job. No need to be like that. I'll let Kevin know I've spoken to yez and there's nothing for him."

"That's fucking better, big man," said John. "Why don't you be on yer way now? There's a good boy."

Fucking condescending Irish prick. Sure I left, but that wouldn't be the end of it.

Back home I got hold of Kevin and told him I would need him for a little job the next night. I also told him to bring along his big box van 'cos we would be taking a little trip down the M6.

I had two of the lads out of the gym with me in the Rover when, just after midnight, we pulled on to the industrial estate and parked up at the back of the McGreeveys' warehouse.

Now, technically, going into the building wasn't playing by the rules, but neither were the brothers. According to them, all the stuff Kevin supplied was seized by the administrator. Well, let's check and see if that was true.

"Right Kev, once we're inside there's a fucking thousand boxes," I explained. "You sure you're going to be able to find your stuff if it's there?"

"No problem, all my packaging has the company logo on," he replied. "Soon as I see it we'll be in business."

We were inside no more than 10 minutes when Kev whistled to say he found what we were looking for.

"It's not all here, Shaun. Got to be about a third of what I delivered missing."

"No problem Kev. We'll just make it up with whatever else you want from the other boxes. Fill yer boots."

It took us nearly an hour to load up the van and, to be honest, it was very tempting to empty the whole place. Should have brought a bigger lorry.

Now a job like this wasn't just going to end with us driving up the road and forgetting about the brothers. They were clearly capable lads and turned over the likes of Kev all the time. Wouldn't surprise me if they had some connections over the water in Ireland. Not for a minute did I imagine they were going to take it on the chin and move on.

No, this was only going to resolve itself by them understanding that when they threatened to make my life unpleasant, they picked on the wrong man. They were tough guys together in the office, but I wondered what they were like on their own at home?

We took the van back to Kevin's place, unloaded it and then I did a quick turn around and headed back down the road to Eccleshall, with one of the lads riding shotgun with me. It was the same routine at the house with the lad out first and then, a few minutes later, John emerged and headed to his Rover.

"Morning, lad," I shouted as I walked towards John. Me mate stood by the car and kept an eye on things.

"What the fuck are you doing here?" he said.

"Nice house, must have cost a few bob, this?"

"Never you fucking mind. You don't seem to have got the message lad. We fucking warned you to stay away."

I always like it when someone confirms they'd been making threats. The recorder on me mobile phone was playing away, so everything John said was being stored.

"You can fuck your fucking warnings," I told him. "You want to have a go at me? Come on now, on yer own or do yez need your fucking brother with ya to hold yer hand?"

Give him his due. He went straight to land one on me but I saw him getting ready to throw it and was way out of range. Quick step to the side and I grabbed him and got him down on the ground. He was a big fucker, but with the hold I had him in, he wasn't going anywhere.

"Now that wasn't very nice was it?" I said as I held him down. "Me mate over there's got his camera going and now we'll have some nice little footage to go with yer making threats. Now do yerself a favour and listen. When you get to work this morning, you won't be surprised to find I've done a little bit of spring cleaning for ya. Had me mate Kevin down with me just to make sure we were cleaning the right stuff, you know, all those duvets he gave ya. Turns out he wasn't happy with the quality of the work so we've taken 'em back, along with some of your other stuff to make up for what we couldn't find.

"Sure you won't be thinking of running to the police or anything 'cos, if I remember, you told me you gave all Kev's stuff to the administrator. And if you're thinking you and yer fucking brother are brave enough to come and see me, bring it on. Don't be thinking about ringing any of yer friends in Ireland either. I've got me own mates over there who I've done business with before. Took them a little while to learn about me."

This had got him thinking 'cos when I put him back on his feet he wasn't saying a word.

"Best we leave things as they are," I said, finishing up. "Say hello to your brother for me."

A couple of days later, I was in the office when me mobile went.

"Is that you Shaun? John McGreevey here."

"Hi, lad. What can I do for ya?"

"Shaun, me and me brother have been speaking to a few

people and thinking about things. We'd be happy to let bygones be bygones if that's okay with you? No hard feelings now, okay?"

"Fine with me. Thanks for letting me know."

Should have gone into the diplomatic service, me. I can calm any troubled waters. Only slight problem was that Kev was still short of cash, but at least he had a mountain of duvets to get rid of. No problem, though, 'cos I had an army of mates used to selling stuff on the quiet. Christ, you couldn't move in the pubs over the next few weeks without someone trying to sell you a duvet!

"Egyptian cotton, duck down, yours for £50, normally go for at least £150."

CHAPTER 23
THE AGENT

I was in the gym one day when this lad, Joey, came over. He's in most days doing weights and keeps himself to himself. No problem with that, of course, 'cos there are plenty of other nutters around to keep life interesting.

I had only spoken to him a couple of times since he started coming, so I was a bit surprised when he asked if he could have a word in private. No problem there so I took him into the office at the back, poured us both a cup of tea and asked how I could help.

Turned out Joey started up his own tiling business a few years ago and it was going well. He began with jobs worth a couple of hundred quid, but over time built his reputation and won a good name with some of the big builders who put some work his way.

It was one of these "favours" that landed Joey in the shit.

He was put in touch with a big-time football agent, who handles dozens of Premier League and Championship players. Now you know how much these fucking superstars earn? Well, think about the agents who set up the deal. For every pound note the player gets, his agent's pocketing 20 per cent. With salaries running into tens of thousands a week, plus bonuses, plus sponsors, there's a fortune coming in. And the agent's scooping his slice off everyone on his books.

The lad Joey was put in touch with was probably worth £100m at least. He built a massive pile in the sticks in Cheshire with 12 bedrooms, an indoor pool, cinema, tennis courts, the fucking lot. And, of course, everything in it was top of the range – nothing out of Ikea within a thousand miles of the place.

Joey thought he landed the jackpot when he got the call to do some work there. Big job, retiling a load of bathrooms. Seems the stuff they already had on the walls and floors was the wrong shade and the agent wanted it all ripped out and done again. Could only have been a couple of years old. What a fucking waste.

The agent wanted to use these special Italian marble tiles that cost around £500 each. By the time all the numbers came in, the bill would be 50 grand, which is normally what Joey took for the whole year.

At first, the job went fine. Joey and the lad he had working with him would do a couple of weeks and stick a bill in at the end for labour and materials. The first time the agent paid, Joey spotted there was an extra £500 in the envelope. He sent a text straight off to the guy thanking him for the tip. But that's when it all started to go tits up.

"What tip?" came the reply.

"The extra £500 you gave me," texted back Joey.

"I didn't give a tip. Bring it back."

Too honest for his own good, our Joey. If he'd kept his mouth shut, he could have pocketed the cash. Instead he had to hand it back and now he knows, despite having everything he could want, the agent is a fucking mean-fisted prick.

He hadn't even said thanks when Joey next turned up at the job. He just took the money and wandered off.

"I kept me head down after that, Shaun," Joey told me. "Took about another six weeks to finish everything off. All the time he hung around but never said a fucking word to me. Nothing about how the stuff was looking, just peering into whichever room we were working in, having a look see and walking off.

"When I stuck the final bill in, I knew there was going to be shit to pay. He owed me more than 30 grand. I wasn't taking the piss – it was a decent price and what we agreed. He looked at the bill and just fucking burst out laughing. All of a sudden, I'm a shit tiler and all the stuff was done wrong. It's all bollocks and he knew it. He offered me £15,000. He's done me like a fucking kipper, Shaun. I maxed out at the bank to do this fucking job and get the right stuff in just like he'd asked. I know it was stupid, but I just took the money, Shaun. There were so many bills piling up I didn't think I had any choice.

"Now he's sitting there in his fucking palace, and I've hardly got a pot to piss in. It ain't right. I've been asking around and some of the lads in the gym suggested you might be able to help. I'd love it if you could mate – anything to see that smile wiped off the prick's face."

Now as you know, I like a good sob story, especially if there's a little pay day at the end of it. Not too much in this case, but maybe a couple of grand if I could persuade the agent to play ball.

Next day, I jumped into me Range Rover – had a few good scores lately so finally got myself a decent motor – and drove down to Wilmslow in Cheshire to pay the agent a visit.

Joey wasn't exaggerating when he said the guy lived in a palace. Fuck me, this place looked like something one of those Arab sheikhs would live in. Makes my place look like a fucking shack. There were even fucking peacocks wandering the lawns. They may look pretty but fucking noisy fuckers those peacocks. Wouldn't want them living next door to me.

I carried on up the drive and parked the Rover next to this spanking new Audi R8, just the thing I'll buy when me lottery numbers come in. Time to do some business first, though.

I threw me jacket on and walked up to the front door. There's no bell, instead just a long golden chain hanging down. Fair enough, I did me Quasimodo bit and gave it a tug. Christ, it was like Big Ben going off at midnight. What with the peacocks and this fucking noise, you'd never get any sleep.

It took another couple of tugs before there was any sign of life. There was a security camera pointing right at me above the door so whoever was inside had a chance to give me the once over before deciding whether to answer.

When the door did open, it was not what I'd expected. It was a woman, sobbing her eyes out and her face was fucking black and blue. Someone gave her a proper battering.

She could hardly get a word out she was crying so much. Fuck the job I came here for, I thought, let's sort her out first.

"Come on love," I said. "Let me help you."

I walked straight inside, put me arm round her shoulders and walked her into the house. She just collapsed into me, holding on for dear life. I walked her into one of the living rooms – gorgeous, of course – and sat her down on one of the sofas. She just sat there for the next couple of minutes, crying her eyes out with me just trying to reassure her everything would be all right.

"Come on girl, tell us what happened, who did this to ya?" I asked when she finally got control.

"I'm so sorry, so sorry," she said, but what the fuck was she apologising to me for?

"Don't be stupid love, just take your time and tell me what happened. I'm Shaun by the way. Nothing to worry about with me. I was just knocking to speak to the guy who owns this place."

I must have said the wrong thing 'cos that sets her off all over again.

"Come on love, calm down, tell me what's happened."

This time I got some answers and it was not a pretty story.

She told me the fella who battered her is the same guy I was looking for. Seems he had a bit of a short temper and could fly off the handle at the slightest thing.

Night before she was watching the telly when he asked her for something but she hadn't heard. Next thing she knew, he was screaming at her, calling her every fucking name under the sun and then let fly with his fists. She tried to protect herself as much as she could, but it turned out he was quite a big fella and she had not been able to fight him off. Now if there's one thing I hate most in life, it's fucking bullies.

First our man picked on Joey and bounced him for fun just 'cos he could. Now he battered his girlfriend. He probably thought she wouldn't ever walk out on him or tell anyone what he did. Why would she when he's got all the money in the world?

The fact she opened the door to me, though, suggested she had had enough. It would have been far easier to leave me pulling on the chain at the front door than invite me inside and confront what had happened to her.

"What time's he home, love?" I asked her. "Think I should have a little chat with him about his behaviour."

"He's not home tonight, Shaun. He's away on business until the weekend."

"Fair enough, if it's okay with you I'll come back then, and we can see what he's got to say for himself. You just tell me what time you want me here and I'll arrive in time for when he turns up. Make sure the kettle's on, though, and if you've got Kit Kats that would be very nice. Now, you go clean yourself up 'cos the way your mascara's run you look like something out of Halloween."

At least I got her laughing when I left, poor love.

I thought about this prick all week, then on Saturday morning me mobile rang and the girl was on the phone. Her fella was landing at Manchester airport in a couple of hours, so if I left in about half an hour, I would have plenty of time to make it down to the house.

Good as gold, when I arrived a little while later, she had the tea ready and even bought some Kit Kats for me. After a couple of days, she looked a lot better – the swelling went down a lot, but she was still wearing a load of make-up to cover up some shocking bruises.

I was sipping away at me tea when the boyo arrived in his own R8 – personalised number plate, of course. He was looking at my Rover as soon as he pulled up, clearly thinking "Who the fuck is this?" as his girl hadn't mentioned anything about visitors.

He walked into the house, dumped his bags in the hall and headed straight to the kitchen where the first thing he saw was me sitting with his missus, laughing away.

"Who the fuck are you?" he shouted. "What's going on?"

"Now, now that's not very nice is it?" I said. "My name's Shaun and I'm a friend of your girl here, just having a cuppa and a bit of a chat. All right?"

He was clearly used to getting his own way in every fucking aspect of his life so finding a cheeky Scouser sat in his kitchen with his missus – and one that looked well capable of handling himself – got him on the back foot. Still, he wasn't ready to play ball yet.

"Who the fuck are you? I know all her friends, and she's never mentioned anyone called Shaun. Tell me who you are and why you're here or I'm calling the police."

"Please do mate. I'm sure they'd love to have a chat with your missus and me. We can tell them what a little piece of shit you are."

"What did you say?" he shouted back. "Right, I'm calling the police now. You're going to be in big trouble breaking in here and threatening me."

"Threatening you? What you on about? I've just called you a few names such as a little piece of shit, which is precisely what you are. And as for breaking in, I think you'll find your lovely lady here invited me in. Just take a look at her phone and you'll see she called me number and asked me to come over."

He started to worry now 'cos he was looking at his missus and she was just stood there beside me, not saying a word but looking like she enjoyed every minute of it.

"Why don't you take a seat, little piece of shit, and we'll have a chat."

I could see he was in two minds as to whether to still go for the phone and ring the bizzies or maybe try and force me out the house. But like all fucking cowards, it's one thing beating up a girl, but a totally different matter when the person facing him could clearly cause him serious damage.

"C'mon, sit down and let me explain a few things," I said.

"Now, I came here on Tuesday hoping for a nice, polite conversation on behalf of a friend of mine. You know him – Joey the tiler, who did all that lovely work for you. All I wanted was to discuss how you could settle the money you owe him – and don't fucking say you don't 'cos we both know that's bollocks. What do I find when I get here, though? You ain't around and it's obvious why 'cos you'd beaten the shit out of your missus. The state I found her in, fuck, what sort of fucking man are you? You want to start throwing your weight around, why don't you come outside with me and we'll see how tough you are? C'mon big man, or are you just a fucking little shit like I first thought?"

He ain't going nowhere. He's sat there shitting himself, and you could see he was terrified. What he doesn't know is he wasn't worth a single slap. I wouldn't soil my hands on a piece of slime like this. He might have the biggest bank balance going, but he ain't got no balls.

"Now here's what we're going to do 'cos I feel in a good mood today and can see a few things need changing round here. First off, you can write me a cheque for 35 grand for Joey, slightly more than you owe him of course, but then I understand you like to tip people. Don't even think about cancelling it after I've gone 'cos I'll just have to come back and have this chat again and perhaps persuade your missus here to ring a lad I know down at the nick and fill him in on how punchy you can be. Took a few pictures of her face the other day, by the way, just to keep as a memento.

"Speaking of your missus, she'd like to call it a day, if that's okay with you? She loved all the money, of course, but at the end of the day having the shit kicked out of her every time you are in a bad mood just doesn't compensate.

"Now I'll leave it to you to work out how much you think she needs to live in the style she's got used to. Feel free to be as generous as you want 'cos I'm sure any price is worth paying to make sure your glorious reputation stays intact."

He didn't need any time to think 'cos paying me Joey's money and getting the girl out of his life is a drop in the ocean with the money he's got in the bank.

Turns out the girlfriend was pretty smart 'cos she spent the last three days clearing all her stuff, and pretty much anything else that wasn't nailed down, out of the house. What with a nice bit of money in the bank, plus her own R8 sat out on the drive, maybe her new life wouldn't be too bad at all.

I gave Joey a call on the mobile on my way back to Warrington, and he was fucking over the moon that I got all his money so quickly. There was even a large tip in it for me.

"To be honest mate, finding out he was beating the shit out of the missus made the job a lot easier," I explained.

"Shaun, you're a fucking genius mate, can't thank you enough," Joey said. "You can keep the extra money mate. You're worth every fucking penny."